Roar!

Roar!
Martin Hayes

smoke

STACK
BOOKS

Smokestack Books
1 Lake Terrace, Grewelthorpe, Ripon HG4 3BU
e-mail: info@smokestack-books.co.uk
www.smokestack-books.co.uk

ISBN 9781999827618

Smokestack Books
is represented
by Inpress Ltd

Printed & bound by ImprintDigital.com, UK

for Victoria

Contents

the men I work with

a man I work with
cries every time it gets too busy
throws his head back onto his fat neck
and stares up into the ceiling
all the while muttering under his breath
how thankful he is that he still has a job
and hasn't been allowed to die yet

a man I work with
goes home every night to make Airfix models
only to hang them from his ceiling
or spread them out across his attic floor
reenacting the battle of Midway
or the siege of Leningrad
talking all day about historical wonders
and what men and women have been capable of before

a man I work with
goes to the toilet every hour
to snort himself out
and comes back
like a Viking halfway through raping himself through a village
only to administer a masterclass in controlling
that text books could be written about

a man I work with
gets so drunk in the nights after his shifts have finished
that when he comes in for work the next morning
he looks as small as a little death rattle
rattling away at his keypad
with eyes that shine through his pain
and a smile on his face
that has no right to exist

the men I work with
haven't written any great books
that everyone talks about
they haven't painted any great pictures
or composed a symphony
that can bring a tear to the eye
but they have worked for years doing 11-hour shifts in a dead-end job
they have spent years getting screamed and shouted at by supervisors
so that those supervisors could feel like they were 8 feet tall

they have spent years tapping away at keypads
sending instructions to couriers to drive their big vans to recently shutdown
offices
to remove desks and chairs still warm from the redundant arses
that used to sit on them earning just enough money to pay their rent years
spent tapping away at those buttons
sending instructions to couriers to whizz through the streets
to collect the blood of a £500 an hour private healthcare patient
and deliver it to a lab so the results can be returned within 45 minutes
as 83-year-old women die in corridors waiting for an extra blanket years
tapping away at those buttons sending instructions
for men to go and pick up the forgotten hat of a pop star
the forgotten shawl of a millionaire actress the forgotten
shoes of a £1,000 an hour model the forgotten bow tie of a CEO
only to drive like lunatics through the streets risking their lives
just so they can get them back into their soft hands years
spent making sure that the documents and contracts of the Great companies
arrive before the deadline
so that padlocks can be snapped shut on the doors of a factory for the last time
and playgrounds
in which they grew up in
in which they drank their first can of beer in smoked their first cigarette in
played kiss chase in
can be turned into building sites where cranes will raise yet another block of
luxury flats
up out of the Earth

these men I work with
who haven't written any great books
painted any great pictures
composed any symphonies
but who
just by the act of living and carrying on
being controllers
help keep the world up in the sky
the birds on wires singing the soil moist in a pair of hands the
flowers and stars burning bright with meaning with those smiles
that have no right to exist
a million times more genuine and stirring
than any of those great pieces of art
could ever be

in the month of January

after a record 18 complaints and two suspensions pending an
investigation
in the month of January
and in response to the supervisor's edict
that the controllers needed to cultivate
better working relationships
with the rest of the workforce
Stevie has given up writing up on the toilet walls
that the telephonists are easy lays
and that Janey from accounts
takes it up the arse
Marcus has stopped mumbling 'dummy' under his breath
every time he is asked by his right-hand man
what Marcus thinks is a particularly stupid question
Phil has given up walking into the recruitment office
and screaming and shouting at them
about the quality of the couriers they are taking on
who don't even seem to know where Buckingham Palace is
never mind Bishopsgate
and Corey and Robbie have stopped jumping off their chairs
the moment they spot one of the beautiful women from sales
walking through the control room
standing there in the middle of the aisle
gently squatting
slowly rubbing the palms of their hands
up and down their hairy thighs
like a pair of Neanderthal men
while sticking their tongues in and out of their mouths
at a furious speed
while the rest of us
have just given up
period

after all
who wants to work in an environment
in which you are not allowed to scream and shout
to take the piss out of and blame
or continually devise ways
in which you can disrespect and dehumanise
your fellow workmates?

a new hot 38-year-old girlfriend

Dermot gets sent pictures and texts on his phone
from his new hot 38-year-old girlfriend
revealing to him her breasts
or detailing what she plans to do to him
when he gets home from his 11-hour shift

Dermot goes around the control room
showing these pictures and texts from his new hot 38-year-old girlfriend
to his fellow controllers
hoping they will understand how lucky he is
and why he is now tired and exhausted
due to her demands on him
in the bedroom
and the hallway
and the kitchen
rather than before
when he was always tired and exhausted
from dealing with all of the abusive texts
and the pictures of bills
that had just dropped through the letterbox
that his ex-wife used to send him

Dermot is still as skint as before
and he still owes the same companies
the thousands of pounds that he owed them before
but it is important for him to let his fellow controllers know
that he is tired and exhausted now
in a different way, for a different reason,
a way that makes him want to smile and share things,
a way that makes him feel proud
to be a man
amongst all of these other
debt-laden men

never beautiful enough

it is sometimes beautiful
to hear the telephonists
talk about the nastiness of their men
as they simultaneously take down jobs
and paint their nails

it is sometimes beautiful
to hear the monsters from sales
talk about their troubled human life
swapping stories about their kids' lack of progress in school
as they smoke cigarettes outside
when only an hour before
they were screaming obscenities at a trainee controller
because the fuck-up he'd been responsible for
had endangered their monthly bonus

it is sometimes beautiful
to listen in on a group of supervisors
discussing the previous weekends' football
as they mouth clichés and platitudes about the games
that real football fans
would never use

it is sometimes beautiful
to hear the mechanics
hungover from the previous night's alcohol and drugs
talk to their fellow mechanics
about their little children
who walked or spoke a word
for the very first time
last weekend

and it is sometimes beautiful
to catch the MD on the phone
overhearing him telling his wife that he loves her
and calling her Bunny

but never beautiful enough

the talented unknown man

the busy afternoons bring jobs down onto the screens
faster than you can get them out sometimes
and the picture becomes confusing for all of us mortals
but Marcus comes alive at these moments
he senses it
he plugs in
and you can see his eyes begin to bulge and sparkle
as he realises that it is his time now
pulling his right-hand man off the box and sitting down
instantly knowing where all of his couriers are
and what they are doing
instantly forming this mental map
of what is going on inside his theatre
somehow managing to straightaway allocate work out to them
that makes sense
jabbering away over the radio like an auctioneer
crafting out runs that link onto jobs that link onto other jobs
so that the jobs momentarily start to disappear from the screen
but they keep coming
as the double-ups and triple-ups and quadrupling-ups become even
more unfathomable
with his body sat leaning forwards in his controller's chair
always relaxed but taught
always cocked but balanced
half-in and half-out of something
his hands moving like lightning across the keypad
for 6 hours solid
until it finally all starts to calm down and the intensity drops
so that he can get up
brushing himself down
handing it all back over to his right-hand man

you can tell the people about their Picassos
and their Dalis
about their Van Goghs and their Rembrandts
and you can build venues
to which they will come
so that they feel like they are in front of awe
but there was no need for us
to take trips down to the Tate or National Gallery
because we had our own artist in residence
carving out masterpieces
on a daily basis

.

Marcus' skill

as Marcus sits at his control point
trying to allocate jobs to couriers
faster than they come in
so that his screen doesn't back up with jobs
he also has to factor in
that he can't just ping out jobs to couriers
willy-nilly
and expect them all to just do what he says

as Marcus sits at his control point
he has to understand
that all of the couriers out there
are self-employed human beings
who rely on him to link and weave
the jobs that keep dropping down onto his screen
into patterns that they,
sat on their motorbikes
or inside the cabins of their vans,
can understand
and which will cause them to do less unpaid miles
when travelling to collect the jobs

Marcus understands
that the thousands of decisions he makes each day affects
EVERYBODY
and his skill
is in being able to make all of it work
so that the clients can think that it was just like buying a can of coke
and the couriers
can get off their bikes
or out of their vehicles of a night
knowing that Marcus
has made it happen for them

Marcus' skill
at being able do this
is what he gets paid for
and what keeps people like Harry, our head supervisor
in their 70-grand-a-year jobs

Marcus' skill
is the guts that makes things able to stick together
that makes things able to happen
that makes things get understood
and bought into

while Harry's
is to take credit for it
and to report back to the Board of Directors
that he has it all
under control

our Marcus and Jimi Hendrix

our Marcus picks up his headphones and places them over his ears
straightening out the mic so that it rests up against one of his
Spartacus cheekbones
rather than a millimetre away from his lips
like the rest of us do

our Marcus sees problems happening
whole minutes before anyone else does
he uses his instinct and mind
to head them off at the pass
sending couriers in early for jobs
or letting them pass scores of other jobs
just so they can get rid of the problem one
and no-one has to suffer
the vile mouth of our supervisors

our Marcus can't talk to our couriers
because what he has to say to them they won't understand
but they all love Marcus more than any other controller
because whenever Marcus is controlling
they end up earning more money
than whenever any other controller is controlling

our Marcus is set apart from the rest of us controllers
because when it is busy on a Friday afternoon
with jobs dropping down onto our screens like confetti
he can clear all of them up
finding couriers and weaving and allocating them such intricate
patterns of jobs
that none of us can see
that it makes all of the noise stop,
he can actually make the noise
suddenly stop,
like he has just placed his foot on the throat of time

our Marcus is cut from the same cloth
as Jimi Hendrix
as Beethoven
as Van Gogh
as Nikola Tesla
they are the ones who move things on, rip up the standards
they drink rainbows and piss solar flares
they eat up black holes and shit stars
leaving the rest of us amazed at their insight
unable to do anything else other than wonder
how many more laws there are in this Universe
that we don't understand yet

a beautiful pair of man-eyes

walking into my first proper control room
it wasn't the heat and chaos
or the people rushing around screaming at everybody
or the pressure that seemed to hang in the air
or the way that everybody in there
seemed so frantically interested
in what was going on
that I remember now

what I remember now
are the eyes of this man
who sat at a desk elevated above everyone else
with 4 massive computer monitors in front of him
showing all of the live jobs
which he then had to send to one of the 5 control points
he thought could best deal with them
and how serenely he remained
above and apart from all of the chaos
how it was so obvious
that he was the one
keeping it all together
sitting there
almost like a Buddha
taking no lunch
never changing his demeanour
or getting rattled
through the whole 11-hours of his shift

they were the first beautiful pair of man-eyes
I had ever seen
and back then
I remember thinking
that if I was ever going to be able to get through
anything
then I was first going to have to learn
how to get a beautiful pair of man-eyes
like them

Stacey

Stacey has dropped hints for the last six months
that she can do this controlling lark better than most of us men
who because we are so tied up with our egos,
letting them run around our minds like dictators hung out on coke,
whenever we make mistakes
we are unable to backtrack and admit our errors
or work out ways to fix them
preferring instead to try and lay the blame off
by screaming and shouting at right-hand men and couriers
who have done nothing wrong,
or huffing and puffing about the stress we are being placed under
which considering,
'it's amazing that we don't make hundreds more mistakes,'
or, and which is her personal favourite,
us blatantly just standing there
as the customer is on the phone yelling at her,
the error clearly visible on the screen in front of us,
with a look of astonishment on our faces,
before us saying, 'I didn't do that,
the system has obviously fucked up again,'
or, 'I didn't allocate that job to that courier
because only a fucking idiot
would do that,'
to which Stacey would just let out a deep sigh once again
before asking resignedly
what the controller wanted her to tell the customer
this
time.

a class act

when Stacey was given the opportunity
to sit on one of the van control points
it didn't go down well with most of the 40 couriers
she was now in control of
as though there were some women couriers out there
the majority of them were men
and they all immediately wanted to know
why there was a woman on the box
controlling them,
calling up their usual controller
and the supervisors
to ask what was going on,
whether they were serious
or just taking the piss,
putting her on there to try and show her up
so that they could maybe pull her down a peg or two

no one actually stopped to think
that this woman might be right
and could do the controlling better
than most of the men in there

so when it was nearing the end of the afternoon
with Stacey still on there
controlling away like a veteran
with very few issues all day
and an above average
stats performance
the phone calls in from the couriers
suddenly stopped

and when Stacey got up after her shift finished
handing over to the next controller
I so much wanted her to turn around
as she walked out of that control room
and give all of those men the finger
shouting back at them,
'take the piss outta that!
you misogynist old fucks!'
but no
Stacey just left
not waiting around for any validation or cheer
as though she had completed just another shift
just like she had always done when she was just a right-hand man
as though it was the most natural thing
in the world,

the way it was going to be
from now on

10,000 miles away from home

those Friday mornings Thiago used to bring in that cheese bread
the controllers immediately dropping everything
the moment he walked in
only to gather round Thiago as he unpacked his rucksack
to get at those 3 tupperware boxes full of that cheese bread
that the controllers had been waiting all week for
and when he unclipped the lid off those boxes
the whole control room would fill up with the smell
of his dead mothers' hands
as Thiago would ask all of the controllers to stand back
so he could bend in and breathe up that smell closing his eyes feeling
the pleasure of the picture that smell conjured up in his mind pour
all over the bones of his back making his hairs stand up him
to squeeze his eyes tighter
so he could feel again his childhood
and the smells of his mother's hands
filling that tin-roofed house with her magic
how nothing ever seemed to be that bad while the smell
of her cheese bread was in the air
even the noise of his younger brothers and sisters fighting
became softer
even those harsh days he spent hauling wood and maize from the fields
until he dripped with sweat and held a thousand cuts in his hands
even they
seemed worth it
when she pulled that cheese bread out the oven
as he'd stand at the door of the kitchen watching her prepare
the rain sounding like the spirits from the jungle
that backed onto their house
had pulled on their biggest boots
and were now dropping down from the trees
trying to explode that tin-roof to get at that smell
as the animals outside took cover under the awning
that leaned out from the kitchen
the two donkeys the only ones tall enough to run their noses

up and down the little gap in the slightly ajar windows
trying to get their bit of that cheese bread into their systems that
system
that Thiago was now reliving
in this control room 10,000 miles away from home
trying to hold onto the feel
of what it meant to him
when he stood out in those fields that spread out their greens as far
as the edges of the world
before he and this new family of his began another 11-hour shift
trying
never to let that way of life die forever
which it never would
while there were still ovens to pull cheese bread out of

then when he'd finished remembering,
breathing in all of that cheese bread,
he'd straighten back up and point at that cheese bread
before announcing to all of his fellow controllers,
'do you know what that is, fellas,
that is
home!'

the controllers knowing then
that it was okay for them to dive in
and rip or tear chunks off of that cheese bread
feed it into their mouths
spending hours afterwards tapping away at their keypads
with the smell of Thiago's mother all over their dirty hands
and Thiago
taking up his position in his controller's chair
with the biggest smile he'd had all week
rooted
right there in his face

so where's my 400 grand?

sometimes
when it was busy
and you had enough couriers out there
to cope
controlling could make you feel
like you were conducting a symphony
in which every note
effortlessly linked into every other note.

the smoothness with which it all flowed
got into you somehow,
it got into your blood and under your nails,
it got into your fingertips and swam through the lining of your guts,
and you could actually feel yourself getting sharper
more alert
and then when the adrenalin kicked in
it lifted you up above the usual cynicism and politics of this job
into a rare place
where the colours on your control screen
became brighter,
where the keys under your fingertips
became softer,
more like nipples,
or at least something other
than the things you usually
just wanted to beat to death.

and when you sat on the bus or walked home
after one of those shifts
you'd feel like you had done something,
like you had helped create a great piece of art
or at least been a part of something
that had momentarily raged against mediocrity,
and then later

twisting the caps off bottles of wine
while sat at the window
looking at the sun setting fire to a blazing sky
you'd wait for the buzz to pass
and reality to set in

which normally would
the moment the lady came in
to remind you that the electricity bill still hasn't been paid,
that the internet connection payment was coming out tomorrow,
that the bank had been on the phone again today
wanting to know when we were going to be paying some more off the
overdraft
and that she had seen on the news
that Damien Hirst had received £400,000
for sticking his balls on a hot griddle.

a controller's image is everything

the controllers come in on Monday mornings
full of stories about imaginary women
that they fucked over the weekend,
they drag themselves through the control room
like men who've just walked out of a desert
pretending to be exhausted
and close to death
chucking themselves down into their chairs
waiting for somebody to ask them, 'what's the matter?'
wincing any time somebody came to close to them
telling them to be careful,
'because she must've been a tiger or something
the way she's opened up my back,'
taking every opportunity
to let their colleagues know
how their tongues feel like the seized-up calf muscle
of a marathon runner,
how their bollocks have never felt so drained,
their cocks so sore,
drinking can after can of Red Bull,
not giving up the charade
until they think everybody
has got the message

obviously
spending your entire weekend
sitting in front of the telly
getting drunk on cider and wine,
reading all of the tabloids and the Racing Post,
doing Channel 4's
Super-Six,
watching X Factor, porn videos
and Ant and Dec,
every now and then sending out
for curry or Chinese,
waiting to see if your lottery numbers come up
without one ring on the phone
and no one to call
is not the sort of image
our controllers feel comfortable with

the bodies of kings

the two bodybuilder mechanics and three bodybuilder controllers
used to bodybuild together at the gym every lunch time and after work
and there was a fierce rivalry between all of them
as they compared bicep circumferences and thigh-muscle circumferences
always with a neon or shit-coloured protein drink in their hands
walking around the control room screwing up their faces in utter disgust
at what their colleagues fed into their mouths
walking around the workshop in t-shirts two sizes too small for them
their biceps and shoulders stretching that material
flexing their muscles every now and then like glistening stallions
under a Kentucky sun
as they spoke in almost revered tones about bench presses
and squats and 120 k-g
as though they were their gods
looking out of those ever decreasing pupils of theirs
and down along their noses
at the drunk controllers
who couldn't get through a night without a drink
coming in looking tired and beaten
wishing the day away
just so they could get at another drink;
at the fat and obese telephonists
who couldn't get through a day without their fix of burger and chips
continually munching away in between on Doritos and cheese balls
and Haribos and chocolate;
at the couriers who had no time for anything else
other than keeping down the 3 jobs they juggled
who only ever wanted to talk about the different ways
they could sell their labour
so that their hands could earn as much money as possible
before they died;
and at the gamer controllers
who rushed home from work after their shifts
to spend 8-hours-solid in front of their screens
trying to fend off an alien invasion of Earth

as the bodybuilders strolled home like panthers
only to sit naked on their beds
with their legs apart up in the air
waxing themselves ripping off every last hair
from their arse-cracks and perineums and scrotums
administering enemas to themselves just before they go to bed
trying to drain every last drop of fluid
out of those bodies of kings

not everyone can be as focused and disciplined
as those bodybuilders though

some of us have fucking lives to live

lifting off like eagles into the sky

the best bits were the Friday afternoons
when the storms that poured down onto our screens all day
suddenly became a trickle
when all the men in there suddenly became excited
as the night and weekend shone at us from the end
of that little bit of tunnel left
Marlon getting up from his controller's chair every fifteen minutes
announcing to everyone, 'there is a lucky lady out there right now fellas,
and she doesn't even know it yet,' as he clapped his hands together
and let out a roar
as Stevie sat back with a big Cheshire-cat grin on his face
rubbing his hands together in anticipation so fast
that smoke rose up from the palms of his hands
as Norm ran up and down the control room aisle faster than usual
his shattered and replaced hip from his motorcycle accident
making him look like a human seesaw
as he played up to his colleagues' laughter
doing that 'ooh-aah, lad' pirate impression of his
as Marcus made paper aeroplanes out of the memos we'd received that day
that Antoine his right-hand man plucked out of that air
and crushed into paper balls
before throwing them back up
letting them fall until they were the exact height for him to smack them
sideways with his hip
before spinning around 1 2 3 times on the spot
all the while firing off imaginary bullets from the fingers he'd shaped into
guns on his chest
as Tony spoke in almost revered tones
about the amount of rosé and beer he was going to drink
before passing out and forgetting everything
as Dermot stood in the middle of the room

stretching and flexing those muscles of his telling anyone
who would listen
that he was limbering up
because he had it on good authority
that he was going to be involved in a 48-hour bout of Turkish wrestling
with his new hot 38-year-old girlfriend

and then there was Ronnie
who would just sit there
with his arms folded and a look on his face
that didn't understand what was going on why
these men he worked with all week who seemed that whole week
to be stuck in that same pit of depression he was always in
were now suddenly lifting off like eagles into the sky
were now talking about this great life they all had
as though the women and beer and wine they were about to ingest
was going to equalise all of that pain
make it all ok
when in reality
they'd all just be back in on Monday
feeling it again

some men
will just never understand
what a Friday afternoon means
to other men

braggarts and liars

when the new fella let it be known
that back in 84
he had taken up Thatcher's offer
and bought his council house overlooking Blackheath
for 140-grand
and that now it was worth
more than 'two million'
it didn't endear him
or make him any new friends
inside that control room

it wasn't that the controllers had any moral disgust
at the buying and selling of council homes
it was more that they now had to remember once again
the time when they were also in that position,
sat safe in that tenancy,
only to have lost it through not contributing to the rent enough
or for getting caught sub-letting it out while living in Thailand
or for drunkenly setting fire to the front room once too often
or for getting banged-up for jacking cars or dealing drugs
or because they got loved-up
and let her have those kids
before it all turned sour
with her remaining on the tenancy
and him walking off into bedsit land

making them all remember once again
when they were in that position
only to fuck it up
could easily have set the new fella up
as a braggart and a liar

but being controllers
they didn't need any reasons for that

being controllers
they'd already learnt to think of the men
that they sat next to each day,
who they counted on to have their backs
and who they drank tequila and beer with
into midnights after their 55-hour weeks,
as braggarts and liars

flight-lieutenant Gordon

Gordon
the new right-hand man
had already been trained by the RAF
at the cost of 500 grand
to be able to fly fighter jets
at speeds close to 500 miles per hour
less than 200 feet
above the Welsh countryside

he also had landed those 25 million pound machines
onto a billion pound aircraft carrier
in the bucking seas of the South Atlantic
and he'd also fired off missiles and dropped bombs
onto strategic targets
in Iraq
and Kuwait
that even he was willing to admit
'most probably killed dozens of people'

so when I gave Gordon
my new right-hand man
a query about a courier trying to deliver to a company
at 32 Wardour Street
that didn't seem to be on the plaque of companies listed in that building
I expected Gordon to be able to sort it out
to be able to understand
that he either needed to look it up on the internet
or else call the client involved
to get a contact number or an email address

10 minutes later
when I turned to Gordon to ask him
what was happening with the query
because I needed that courier
to go on to another job
I was confronted by his blank face
which had obviously not understood
what he had been asked to do
in the first place

500 grand
I guess
is enough to spend training a man
to be able to press a button
that fired off missiles and dropped bombs on people
but nowhere near enough
to arm him with enough common sense
to make him a good right-hand man

flood watch

when it rains harder than it usually does
the man sitting at the end of the control bench
is asked by one of the supervisors
whilst trying keep tabs on 35 couriers and 500 jobs
to also keep an eye
on the top left hand corner of the office
in case any water should start leaking in onto the computers
and that if it does
then to give him a shout

after the supervisor has handed out the task
he walks away muttering something about flash fires
and what rain can do
if allowed to pour over an already creaking
hardware system
especially considering that it is plugged into sockets
that hang loose from the wall

it was good to know
that even in times of danger
our supervisors knew how to keep everybody
relaxed and focused
on their work

my shit little poems

Harry, our head supervisor, pulled me into his office
to ask me how I would feel about being transferred
to Phoenix Express' office in Slough
because if I continue to let the jobs under my supervision
run later than the SLAs we have agreed with our clients
then that was precisely what was going to happen
adding that he didn't give a flying fuck
about the hardware and software not being up to scratch
because he thought, as a controller, I needed to find ways
around those obstacles
and that in fact,
if the truth be told,
I had actually developed an unhealthy relationship
with the operating system I relied on to get out those jobs
continually going on about the 101 ways
it stutters, freezes then crashes
like a little snivelling snotty-nosed school kid
rather than just getting on with it
and working out ways to get around it
like a man
which, by the way, I am paid to be.

as I got up to leave
he finished off by telling me
that if I feel I am being mistreated
and misunderstood yet again,
'then to put that
in one of your shit little poems
you mug.'

well here it is Harry
you dangerous cunt
and I've written a few more
about you too.

calling in sick

Harry, our head supervisor, isn't very tolerant or sympathetic
to days taken off due to illness.
if ever you have to go into him
to let him know that a member of staff
or a particular courier
has called in sick
he grunts
and raises his eyebrows up in disbelief.
when you tell him that you think
he or she is telling the truth,
that they sounded genuine on the phone,
he leans back in his massive swivel-chair and looks at you
as though you are a naïve twit.
'what?' you ask.
'of course they sounded fucking genuine,' he says,
they've had years of practice at it.
what was it this time?
some kind of cancer I bet?
I've heard about dead dads, dead kids,
kids with leukaemia, kids with meningitis,
wives who've had a miscarriage, wives who've been beaten up,
wives who've discovered a lump on their breast, wives
discovered in bed with other men, wives who've left them
with a screaming kid in their arms. I've heard
them all. I've heard everything,
including malaria, bird flu and cot death.
nothing surprises me or shocks me anymore
apart from the truth
which I have found through my years of experience
to be absolutely fucking nowhere near
what comes out of a courier's mouth.'

cynicism and disbelief were rife in a supervisor's mind
at the best of times
but when it came to illnesses
and reasons for days off sick
that's when they really could show
how much humanity
they had been able to lose.

letting the cat out of the bag

at our once a month controllers' meeting
Harry, our head supervisor, told us
that we didn't really want a hardware system
that didn't crash at least 4 times a day
that we didn't really want a software set up
that could actually cope with the 300 jobs per hour
that poured in at us every busy afternoon
that we didn't really want our bonuses to be passed
effortlessly every month
or the toilets to be clean
or our 60 minute lunch hours back
that had recently been reduced to 40
he told us
that we didn't want to be
pulled to one side every now and then
to be told that we we're doing a good job
that we didn't really want
more than 20 days paid holiday a year
or an HR department that would take our grievances seriously
then when he had finished telling us what we didn't want
he stood up
and sent his forearms
down into the desk
his fists clenched
his body just about managing to stay behind its motion
like a silverback
resting on the catapults of its finger joints
and he screamed at us, 'AND DO YOU KNOW WHY?
DO YOU KNOW WHY NONE OF YOU REALLY WANT THAT?'
we looked at his bulging eyes,
we stared at his angry mouth,
we checked that our balls were still there,
'BECAUSE YOU ARE ALL
PUSSIES!
BECAUSE YOU ARE ALL

BEATEN
MEN!
BECAUSE
IF YOU GOT ALL OF THAT
THEN YOU'D HAVE NOTHING LEFT
TO MOAN ABOUT!

THE POINT TO ALL OF YOUR LIVES
WOULD BE TAKEN AWAY!
WITHOUT ANYTHING TO MOAN ABOUT
YOU WOULD CEASE TO EXIST!'

that night after our shifts finished
we all went over the road for a beer
and discussed if we should write a letter to the directors
questioning the tactics Harry had used
at the meeting
how he might be a bit of a loose cannon
a danger to the status quo
putting all of the cards on the table like that
calling our bluff
single handedly motivating us
'the workforce'
by making us think a little bit more about ourselves
than we usually did
was a dangerous game

value for money

the CEO let it be known
that he thought that he wasn't getting enough value for money
out of his controllers.

he thought that the £400 take-home cheques
that he signed over to us controllers each week,
which we put towards paying our rent
and our council tax
and which bought our food
and contributed towards our bills
and our debt,
was too much for what we did
and that he should be getting a whole lot more out of us
for his money.

no one knows where he got this idea from
or how far he thinks £400 a week goes
living in London,
but the CEO isn't happy
and has told his supervisors to find ways
in which we can contribute more.

the supervisors are also unsure what else we can do,
as they tell us at the end of month controllers' meeting,
apart from us
having to do more.

all of us leave the end of month controllers' meeting
feeling confused.

'maybe we should offer to wash his Bentley,' Dermot says,
as we light up cigarettes outside.
'maybe we should offer to iron his suits,' Tony says.
'maybe we should offer to swap places with him for a week
to see how he gets on with our budget
and how we get on with his,' Nigel says.
'no, we can't do that,' Marcus says,
'because if that happened
then he'd realise just how lucky we are
working for a prick like him.'

it was finally agreed,
we would all go back to our bedsits and flats
to work out what we could do more
in our 55-hour weeks
to justify keeping hold of these controlling jobs.

somebody
was going to have to make the CEO feel better
about signing off those £400 cheques
to the men who kept his 22 million pounds a year company going
that was for sure.

all we know is

we will never know what is inside the brain of the CEO
who owns this company we all work for
we will never know from where or why
he makes these decisions about our bonuses getting stopped
or why our overtime rate
is so derisory
we will never know what it is like
to twist a pair of rugby ball cufflinks
so that they are positioned perfectly straight
on the ends of a £300 shirt
or what smoking a £50 cigar feels like
we will never know what it is like
to put our foot down on an accelerator pedal
that shoots a Bentley off down the road
at close to what feels like security
or how it feels
making a decision
that will squeeze a man in a fist until he pops
or how it feels
firing off an email to HR
telling them that 7 human beings will not be needed anymore
and need to be processed off the premises
as cheaply as possible

all we do know
is that the men we all work with
are the same as us
that they have to pay the same bills as us
because if they don't
then their roof will be taken away
and then the love of their woman will be taken away
all we know is that we continually worry
about keeping our jobs
just like you do
because if we didn't have them

then there wouldn't be any food on the table
or shoes for the children's feet
or an internet connection
or laughter and wine

all we know is
that the CEO who owns this company we all work for
is not worried about what we know anymore
because he has reached such a lofty level
that he can't even hear us
and even if he pulled the hearts out of half of his staff's chests
or immolated the twenty best workers of the 400 he employs
then it would affect him and his family
by less than 0.1%

and that, unfortunately
isn't readily taught in the schools
but only learnt
or told
in poems and songs
like this one

before and after

before the takeover
whenever we needed a new pen or notepad
or a new reel of sellotape
we just had to walk in to see Janey in accounts
who had the key to the stationary and cleaner's cupboard
where she would find the item we were asking for
make a note of it in the stationary log
then hand it over to us.

now
after the takeover
whenever we need a new item of stationary
we have to submit a request to our head supervisor
either by email or on one of the new Stationary Request Forms,
which are rarer and harder to find
than rocking horse shit,
which they will then evaluate
before either submitting it to the stationary department,
which, by the way, is still Janey in accounts
with the same key to the same cupboard,
or else rejecting it
and marking it down as 'no further action'
also known before the takeover as
'putting it in the bin'.

if it is accepted Janey will pick the item
before sending you an email the moment the item is ready to collect,
that way it minimises time spent away from your control point
raising productivity
and reducing any chance meetings in the corridors
where plans can be hatched.

the takeover was trumpeted as
'a giant leap forwards for Phoenix Express,
a partnership which will launch us onto the national stage
and secure not only hundreds of jobs for the long term future
but also our position as the number one courier company
in London.'

it was our first exposure
to what the future was going to be like,
full of grandiose plans stunted by bureaucracy,
which was fine
just so long as you didn't need to write anything down
or stick anything back together again.

132 more

the new boss from the company behind the takeover
came in to give us all a pep talk
to ease the uncertainty and fears we all had
of maybe losing our jobs
and to paint for us all a vision
of the future

in groups of ten
we were all given a time slot
when we had to be in the boardroom
to listen to this man

this man who had never made a delivery to anyone anywhere
this man who whenever he got a parking ticket or CCTV fine
had only to make sure that it was entered correctly onto his expense
account
this man who had never had to also hold down a weekend job
hauling 20lb boxes of frozen lamb into the backs of trucks
for £6.50 an hour after tax
just so he could afford to take his kids to the cinema
this man who had the charm and charisma of a politician
rather than the blunt edges of a worker
this man who smiled at us and looked at us straight in the eye
and told us that we were important
what he liked to call 'the oxygen of this company'
which his shareholders had bought
and how it just wouldn't make any sense
to get rid of any one of us
would it?

this man who 6 months later
made the decision on behalf of his shareholders
to shut down our workshop
laying off 7 mechanics
so that all of the repairs and maintenance of our vehicles
could be done by the new companies already existing network
of garages and service centres

this man who lives away in the country
off with the fairies
who is placed under so much pressure
every minute of the day by his shareholders
to increase the bottom line
slowly stripping away all of his humanity and heart
so that with one swoosh of his pen
he can turn upside down 7 people's lives
and still sleep at night
and still play frisbee with his kids on a beach
knowing that he has lied
to 132 more

the 132 left

the 139 people that this man lied to
sat in that big boardroom
convincing us all that we were 'the oxygen of this company'
only to shut down our workshop 6 months later
laying off 7 of us 139
has left the 132 left
wondering which one of us will be next.
132 people who have flesh and teeth and bones to support
but who are now unsure
whether they will be able to do that come the end of the month,
come the next electricity bill,
come Christmas.
132 people who combined
have given more than one million hours of their time
getting paid to inflate this company into something strong,
who have the scars and addictions,
the lonely lives and debts
to prove it.
132 people who now know
that they were lied to by this man
in that boardroom,
on that day when he came in and looked us all in the eye
and told us that we were
the 'oxygen of this company'.

going long periods of time
without any oxygen
is ok for whales, dolphins
and escape artists
but a little bit more tricky
for 132 men and women
who need to know for how long they will be allowed to breathe
if they want to continue paying their rent.

for twelve years these hands...

for twelve years we have been making sure that this client's documents
have been picked up and arrived on time
for twelve years we have been sitting
in these big comfortable controllers' chairs
prioritising this client's bookings
listening to our supervisors tell us that this client
spends enough money a month on couriers
to keep more than half of this control room
in work
for twelve years we have been making sure
that this client is looked after
because we wanted to keep hold of our jobs
and wanted to keep the couriers and other controllers
in their jobs
for twelve years we have done this
only for tonight to see on the news
that this client has been caught with its hands dipped in a pot of blood
overseeing contracts and driving deals
that eventually moved on bombs and mines
to people in countries far away
almost legally
for twelve years our hands have helped do their handiwork
picking up and delivering their menaces
not knowing that men and women and children got blown apart
because these hands,
which only ever wanted to keep hold of their jobs,
made sure that this client's contracts arrived
and got signed
on time
so that they could release the bombs
set the mines
and count the money

we help these corporations exist as our 83-year-old mothers remain in pain

we help these corporations exist by making sure
that the documents of their various deals and contracts arrive on time
we help these corporations exist
as we work through toothache
work through hangovers
pumping away at our keypads
so that the documents they send out
get there on time
and the contracts they need
can be proofread
before being sent back
to be signed
we are told by our supervisors
that these corporations spend enough money on couriers in one year
to make all of our jobs safe

we help these corporations exist
as our 83-year-old mothers have to fill out 28-page forms
to see if they qualify for meals on wheels
as our 83-year-old mothers
who held down jobs for over 60 years
shit themselves on their own because the home help has been stopped
and they are too embarrassed to call a family member in to help
as our 83-year-old mothers sit in homes unable to move
or pick up their grandchildren
because they have been refused an operation
to alleviate their chronic arthritis
by a government who has received millions of pounds
from these same corporations
that we slog our guts out for each day
helping to get their documents and contracts delivered
so that they can remain healthy
and strong

the blood and smiles yet to be delivered into this world

we move the beds of shut down hospital wards
that our grandparents laid in to die
we carry the blood of children still open on operating tables
from blood banks to theatres
just to see if they will live
we pack transit vans full of cakes
and take them to weddings where daughters will be given away to men
we pick up contracts from big lawyers and deliver them to CEOs who
work from home
so that they can proofread them and sign off the building of a dam
that will shut down a river and turn villages into dust
we tap away at keypads all day sending instructions to couriers
to drive their big vans to bankrupt companies
so that they can empty them of the desks and chairs
that workers once sat in
earning just enough money to feed their families and pay their rent
we pick up artificial limbs from factories and deliver them to hospitals
so that men who lost a leg in a war 5,000 miles away
can learn to walk again
we place couriers outside big banks at 2 am
in case the money markets in countries far away take a dive
or soar into the sky
we pick up hearts at road traffic accidents
and rush them off to clinics
so that they can be frozen before they stop beating
we put barrels of ink into the backs of vans
and deliver them to printers in Truro and Dunfermline
so that they can print eviction notices and final demand notices we move
dead people's bodies
after they have been stripped of their organs
and sewed back up as a mark of respect we pick up
projectors screens whiteboards brochures lecterns
and deliver them to conference rooms in hotels
so that a man from one of the big banks can stand in front of 200 people
and explain to them why more and more acquisitions

and the swallowing up of jobs
is the best way to grow and thread a corporation through
with steel and strength

and when our shifts have finished
we go home to play with our daughters and sons
picking up plastic tea pots
pouring imaginary tea into plastic cups while sat at imaginary tea
parties we make
big engine noises come out of our throats
as we help them steer their toy trucks
to the piles of wooden blocks
that they load onto those trucks and steer back across
to the other side of the room
where they unload them and announce to their world that
'everything has been delivered'
where we pick up bottles of wine after they have gone to bed
and sit at a window wondering about the industries of men
and the blood and smiles that are still yet to be delivered into this world
whether or not they will be the ones
to write that song or poem, start
the revolution
that will change everything

exactly how they want it

some of the men here have worked so many years
inside control rooms
that they have come to regard the supervisor's overt aggression,
storming up to them in front of everyone
and calling them a useless idiot,
as normal.

through the slow roasting and turning over the heat
inside this control room for years
some of the men here
have become so used to the tiredness and emptiness
they continually feel
that they have assimilated it into their lives
and now just regard it
as a part of their personality.

some of the men here have spent so many years in debt
unable to get past the third week of any month
without having to concoct some kind of plan,
ask some kind of favour
or else go without,
that they have come to think that this feral approach to money
and the lies they have to tell to get more
is perfectly normal.

some of the men here
have lost some of the most beautiful women in the world,
some have lost their health
their council tenancies
their children
their pets
their Mojos
their pride
and their dignity.
some of them here have lost so much in fact

that they have been conditioned to think
that being a no-one
with nothing but a drink problem
and an empty heart
is exactly how it should be.

impending disasters

we knew the pressure of the job was taking its toll on Martyn
when he started overeating
suddenly going from one coffee and a croissant for breakfast
to consuming 3 or 4 bacon butties and a 6-pack of caramel swirls,
munching all day on chocolate bars
or throwing back handfuls of M&M's into his mouth,
coming back from Sainsbury's at lunch time
with a big bag of food in his hands
only to destroy the whole lot
in the half-hour left of his break.

we knew the pressure of the job was taking its toll on Norm
when his face began erupting in boils
and his skin began to flake off his face
floating down onto his desk
revealing weather-worn-red patches of exposed flesh
which Norm couldn't help but itch
until his whole face became one gigantic sore.

we knew the pressure of the job was taking its toll on Shaq
when his once amiable and polite character
suddenly disappeared over the course of one December
only to be replaced by an angry snarling and swearing Shaq
who had lost his facility to absorb
and now went around chucking things across the control room,
screaming and shouting about how useless this and useless that
everybody was.

we also knew that the pressure of the job
had slowly eaten its way into Tony
when his usual calm poker face
suddenly developed a twitch
which though started off as an occasional impulse
every now and then
had now become a once every five minute event
causing him to also rapidly twitch-blink his eye
while his shoulder moved furiously up and down
inside its socket.

signs are always there
of impending disasters,
it's just at Phoenix Express
no one ever seems to do anything
about them.

as death moves every second a bit closer

last month we were asked to move the contents of one office
into another office
we didn't moan
or get on the phone to HR
to ask if removal tasks were in our contract
because that would have been petty and silly
and besides
if we had
then we would have been singled out as troublemakers
so all of us who were asked to help move the contents of one office
into another office
did exactly what we were told
first we took the smaller items
like the pens pencils and rubbers
the paper bin the stapler the whiteboard
and we removed them from one office
into the other office
then we all pulled together
and got the desk in our hands
and we tilted it up into a shape that would fit through the office door
and then again into another shape that would fit through
the new office door
and then we went back for the filing cabinets
which we heaved and pushed
from one office
into the other office
although one of the controllers caught his hand in between
the door frame
and one of the filing cabinets
which broke his skin and caused him to bleed
but he just screamed out 'fuck!'
and then sucked on his wound continually
as he carried on moving things from one office
into another office

when we had finished
the old office was bare and creepily different
like a room whose occupant had just died
but the other office was full of stuff
and ready for somebody to do some work in it

it's been 5 weeks now
and the new office still hasn't an occupant doing any work in it
but it is ready
and we made that happen
as death moves every second a bit closer

this job has us in its mouth and is shaking us about in its teeth

this job has us in its mouth and is shaking us about in its teeth
as we stumble from one bill to the next
just about managing to keep food on the table
and a roof over our heads
apart from the last week that is
because that's when we have to start with the lies
the borrowing
the asking of favours
that all put together
hopefully will produce just enough
to get us over the line
and into the next month

this job has us in its mouth and is shaking us about in its teeth
as we stumble from one hangover to the next
trying to balance the drinking so that it has as little effect as possible
on the job
the woman
the kids
and our hearts
that seem to want to just pump their way out of our chests
as our minds can't face anything else
other than another drink
another taste
of that freedom

this job has us in its mouth and is shaking us about in its teeth
as debt runs through us like streams of poison
debt: who takes us for walks in the park never letting go of our hand
debt: who always sits next to us on the bus even though it's half empty
debt: who just wants more company
who just wants more attention
and more debt
on offer like a can of Coke
on offer
for us to slip our wrists into

this job has us in its mouth and is shaking us about in its teeth
as only our guts allow us to hold on;
those guts
that pull us up off the floor
that make us feel strong
and unbeatable
that we carry around with us
inside our stomachs
and our fingertips
that make us laugh
feel lucky hold
glasses of wine and beer in our hands dance
with our women and children around in circles
as we all throw our heads up in the air
see
the entire Universe up there
on our side
with the sea and the stars in our eyes
and that unbeatable laughter
to prove it

Rise

the job grinds people down
until they feel like bits of dust,
the job they have to keep hold of
like a dying sparrow in their hands
grinds people down

all of the hours spent dipping their shoulder
and charging at the sun
carrying this dying little sparrow
in their hands
has made them feel bone-tired,
they are exhausted
and close to giving up

the dying little sparrow has almost killed them,
the bills the CCJ's
the rent arrears utility bills dentist bills internet payments
food roof beer shoes shirts, all of it,
has almost killed the very centre of them

the fear of losing everything
has made them supple enough
to accept
almost anything

but only almost
because the holding of hands with a woman under a blood-red sun
and the wine that drips down from rib to rib
to form puddles in the gut
and the music
that lifts sparrows up
back onto their feet,

makes them want to rise,
burst out of hands,
head towards the sun, sit
on wires tin roofs chimney pipes
to sing sing sing
about that unconquerable little bit of them,
how that will never die
like a little sparrow in a pair of hands
however tightly they squeeze it

Big Bri

Big Bri invited all of us controllers
and all of his fellow couriers
round to his house one Sunday
for a barbeque.

the sun was up and hot as Big Bri
entertained all of us who turned up
on the green below his block of flats
telling us stories about his smuggling days
and his hooky gear days
disappearing sometimes
only to reappear wearing his wife's nightie
and her pink satin shower cap
treating us all to his rendition of
I Want To Break Free
which he sang into the shower brush
he heldin his right hand.

Big Bri
who had bought up half of Iceland's beer and wine
and half of their burgers and chicken
just for this one event,
who had a heart like a nuclear reactor
making everything within a 100 yard radius
glow and feel warmer,
who had a laugh that started off in his gut
and rose up through his body
only to explode out of his mouth
loud enough and genuine enough
that it must've made all of the angels in heaven
turn their heads.

Big Bri
who told us there
while sat on that green drinking his lager
and eating his barbequed chicken
that the only reason his wife June
had remained married to him,
had remained able to put up with him,
was because in the 18 years he'd been a courier
he'd never once taken a day off sick
because that is how he is
how he is made
which was to work.

Friday afternoons

the joy of Friday afternoons knowing that
it will only be 3 or 4 more hours
before our shifts finish
and we can walk out of there
with our minds tingling
and all of the wild blood
everywhere

the sudden buzz
that ignites at around 3 or 4 o'clock every Friday afternoon
like somebody has just flicked on a switch

the laughter and jokes
that get a little bit louder, a little bit
riskier
as we can smell the weekend
now marching uncontrollably forwards
just on the other side of that little hill

the beauty we start to feel inside ourselves proud
that our minds
and the fingertips that are a part of our hands
have driven a sword through another one of their weeks
without this body they are attached to
losing its job

those Friday afternoons
when the jobs that kept pouring down onto our screens all day
suddenly become a trickle,
when the buzz of having to double-up and treble-up
and weave jobs into patterns that work
is replaced by the buzz of the upcoming weekend
leaving a control room full of men so heated up by anticipation
that all of the atoms inside us start to move about faster
until they get so close to boiling point

that we can see for the first time
that the Earth is now round again
that we can see for the first time
why the apple fell onto Newton's lap
that we can see Mark Anthony's face
while he was giving it to Cleopatra
feel the fingers of Beethoven
moving over those keys
until it all comes so perfectly together
the moment we put our foot outside that door
and walk up that road
feeling like Beowulfs
out looking for our Grendels

freedom and chains

every Friday night
between the hours of 7 and 8pm
the first cap of the first bottle of wine is opened
the first draught of the first beer is pulled
thus beginning
the slow methodical forgetting process
known as freedom.

the participants,
who try to drink the trembling from their guts
the fear from their eyes
and the memories from their minds,
are not volunteers in this weekly event
they have chosen this way
it is called
their freedom.

and then every Monday morning
between the hours of 4 and 6am
the whistles from their factories
wake them up again,
but having gone through
the slow methodical process
of forgetting everything
they have forgotten everything,
gladly putting their chains back on,
forgetting completely once again
about freedom.

and because this happens on a rotational basis
no one is ever chained for too long
or free for long enough
to do anything about it.

mark Dexter's words

Dexter, the old-timer
floats around the control room
like a leaf caught on the wind

before his shift starts
he fiddles and fusses around his control point
tidying up and polishing the mess left behind by the previous controller
tut-tutting at the lack of respect the new controllers have
for a man's working station
muttering on about how back in the day
Big John or Rattlesnake
'would've carved you up
if you'ld left their control point looking like this'

Dexter
who nearly always started off his sentences with the words
'you mark my words'
before launching into some kind of prediction about the future
how much worse it was going to be than the past
how the brainwashing of the people
'always having their heads stuck in some kind of computer
or mobile phone'
was turning them all into robots
who one day won't even be able to get up of a morning
without plugging in first
who one day won't even own their own thoughts
because everything would've been taken over
and they will have missed it
just because they couldn't be bothered to lift up their heads
from those mobile phones
who one day won't even know what a real sunset looks like anymore
or ever be able to identify again
that electricity feeling in the air
just before a storm hits
who one day won't even know

the difference between a lemon shark and a great white
because they will all have disappeared from our oceans
and everybody would've missed it
just like what's happening to our jobs
'you mark my words'

Antoine's favourite word

Antoine's favourite word was pussy,
everything he did and everything that was done to him
he referenced
to pussy,
he'd sit there adequately fulfilling his right-hand man duties
and whenever a telephonist came in
to ask where this bike was or that van was
Antoine would give them the information they needed
before leaning over and whispering into his controller's ear
that he thought that lady
had a 'sweet smelling pussy',
and whenever one of the couriers got on the phone
and started shouting and screaming at Antoine
because his controller wasn't giving him enough work
Antoine would sweet talk him around
before leaning over and telling his controller
that that courier obviously hasn't had any pussy
in a long long time,
and whenever one of the supervisors
came out and bollocked Antione's controller
for running late on a job
Antoine would wait for the supervisor to walk away
before tapping his controller on the shoulder
and telling him not to worry
because it was obvious that that supervisor
was a pussy,
and other times
when a supervisor came out
and bollocked his controller for not notifying a customer
that their job was running late
the controller would let rip at Antoine
for not covering his arse

before Antoine
after letting the dust settle a little
would suddenly say to his controller
that he needed to chill out
and not take it out on him
just because he wasn't getting any pussy
at home.

everything was
pussy
pussy
pussy
to Antoine
while everything else
just didn't seem relevant.

Antoine the pussy hunter

as I tried to keep my cool
making decisions about which couriers should get the jobs
that kept pouring down onto my screen
knowing that one mistimed allocation
could mean that the balance could tip
causing a client to get on the phone
complaining that the service they were paying for
had gone wrong
Antoine, my right-hand man
whistled old Trojan tunes and spoke continuously
about the differences in the anatomy
of the women he had made love to

as I tried to keep up with the incoming
making sure I kept enough couriers in the 'hot-places'
that could book jobs that would descend onto my screen
like napalm
Antoine, my right-hand man
would be picking dirt from his fingernails
while balancing a phone in between his shoulder and ear
trying to convince receptionists
that even though their courier was running late
it would be a good idea
to go out on a date with him

Antoine, with his slicked back hair and Jamaican accent
could sweet talk accounts back
that were way over the line of dead
and he laughed at all of us controllers
as we flayed away at our keypads
trying to make sure that nothing ever came back on us
concentrating our whole beings
on allocating out the work
while Antoine's whole being
concentrated on just one thing
which was where his next piece of pussy
was coming from

Nigel's breakdown

after receiving a personal call
Nigel has had to get up from his control point
and go into the supervisor's office.

he is in there with his head in his hands
crying his eyes out.

one of the supervisors comes out
and tells us that someone needs to jump onto Nigel's control point
to cover for him
while they sort this situation out.

it isn't long
before Nigel's fellow controllers start speculating
on why Nigel is sitting inside the supervisor's office crying,
on why he has broken down
and is now holding his head in his hands,
and it isn't long after that
before they start up a book
with a £5 stake
and a winner takes all jackpot.

Stevie's bet is that he's most probably heard
that his dog, Bonzo, has been run over,
Mikey's bet is that it's because he's found out
that his missus has been making out
with another guy,
Dermot's bet is that it's because his mother
has found all of his sex toys under his bed,
Robbie reckons it's because a family member, like his mum or aunt,
has passed away,
Ronnie places his fiver on Bonzo the dog
having chewed up his Crystal Palace season ticket

while Antione thinks
that whatever it is
it will almost certainly have something to do
with pussy.

after a while Nigel walks back out with red eyes and hunched frame
to pick up his bag
and walk out of the control room
saying nothing.

Harry, our head supervisor, comes in soon after
and tells us that Nigel has received some bad news
which he needs to go home and deal with
and that we will need to cover his control point
for the rest of the day.

everyone agrees that Mikey has obviously won
but Antoine is not having any of it,
he reckons he should also have some claim
on a percentage of the pot
because, Antione says,
'this just so obviously stinks
of pussy.'

the decision

how do you explain to a man
who has spent 12 years
grinding out 11-hour shifts,
who in all of that time
has never taken a day off
sick,
who has taken that job home with him
every night
and carried it around with him inside his head
every weekend
so that all he has become
is this job

how do you explain to a man
whose pride in being a man
has meant that he has never knowingly allocated a job
to any courier
other than the best one for it,
who has spent scores of his own hours
creating a manual
which he brings in
and shows to all of us other controllers
detailing the protocols and systems we need to adopt
if we want to be a fair and just controller
like he is,
who has taken on the chin
all of the lost bonuses
and all of the forgotten hours he has spent after his shift
covering controllers
who couldn't turn up
because they didn't need this job
like he did

how do you explain to this man
that he is being made redundant
because Phoenix Express is cutting back
on controllers
and not expect this man
to tip up the HR manager's desk
before breaking down
and refusing to move
until he has had this decision
explained to him
by the supervisors he has worked under
for the last 12 years
and who he has saved the skin of
countless times before
rather than by an HR manager
who has only been with the company
for 2 months

down time

when the operating system we rely on to get out these jobs
has been a bit more temperamental than usual
we are let known by our supervisors
that the whole system will be going down for 20 minutes
while the IT guys
away in the new building across the road
dial in
to try and diagnose the problem

during this down time
it is a chance for the controllers to sit back and contemplate
why a company turning over 22 million pounds a year
continues to have so many issues
with its hardware and software systems
but most of them don't bother
most of them prefer to use this time instead
to show one another their increased bicep circumference
or their latest tattoo
most of them chose this time
to drive in the meanings of the various spoofs and cusses
they have been guilty of
while others lean back in their big controllers' chairs
and stick one of their iPod earphones into their ear
carrying on conversations with their colleagues
about how dirty and begging-for-it their woman was last night
or about how mental their woman is or how
if it wasn't for their woman
then they would've left this job years ago
and gone and travelled and fucked their way around the world
like they'd always dreamed

after the system comes back up
the controllers put their tattoos and earphones away
and get back down to allocating out the work

who needs contemplation time
when you've got biceps and music
spoofs and cusses
and women to blame
for almost everything

non-essentials

after a weekend with average temperatures of -2
and rain all of Sunday night
Merv, the overnight and international controller
opened up the shutters in the yard at the rear of the building
only to find icicles hanging from the counter
and from the metal trolleys
that had been pushed up under the windows

the rain that had leaked in and all of the condensation
had finally frozen and hung there
glistening through the cold-teared-eyes of Merv

there was no heating to put on anymore
as during the recent refurbishment
no provision had been made
for such things
because it was deemed a 'non-essential'
to the running of this 22 million pounds a year company
Merv had worked
16 years for

Merv switched on his computer
opened up his email
and sent one off to all of the senior management
wanting to know if they thought he was
a fucking reindeer

school assembly

up on the notice board
they have put a detailed analysis
of last month's attendance records.

each member of staff is listed
and beside their name
they had been given a percentage point
followed by a gold, silver or bronze star
besides which was a big red number
which displayed how many days
each member of staff
had taken off that month,
then after that
there were 30 columns,
one for each day of the month of September,
in which each one was either a tick
or a cross.

it was a mighty report
which must've taken at least a day
of the 160-grand-a-year HR department's time
just to compile.

at the end of the month assembly,
as the headmaster read out the winners
of the three £20 Sainsbury's vouchers,
some of the kids scrunched up pieces of paper
and chucked them at each other
while others blew chewing gum bubbles out of their mouths
and let them loudly go pop
while all of the rest
just stared off into the distance
day dreaming about what they wanted to be
when they grew up.

no difference

the difference between working for Phoenix Express
against any other company
is that Phoenix Express doesn't even pretend
to give a toss

continually dreaming up just-out-of-reach targets
for their controllers to hit
if ever they want to actually receive
their monthly bonus

continually putting up just a little-bit-to-high-a-walls
for the distasteful to climb
if ever they want to go for a promotion
and earn a little bit more money

continually moving the goal posts
and changing the rules for offside
catching the couriers out time and time again
so that they lose hard-earned paid miles
and attendance bonuses
until they finally have no choice
but to leave

the supervisors and managers
continually nipping away at the staff
keeping them in varied states of paranoia
or 'on their toes' as they prefer to call it
so that those same staff
have to take home with them after their shifts
the sound of those voices and those attitudes
constantly reminding them that they are 'pieces of shit'
whose 'jobs are on the line'
so that they drink too much wine
smoke too much dope
argue with their women

speak to their God at the bottom of their bed
or put a fist through a plate-glass window
just to quieten their unease
and paranoia

the difference between working for Phoenix Express
against any other company...
is probably not that much
come to think about it

work work work

you work for 11-hours a day
put your shifts in
you work for your life
and your family
your kids
and the electricity bill
you work for the council tax
and your debt
you work work work
lest it will all be taken away from you
by men who place rings on the fingers of whores
by men who've put a blanket around the vastness of Jupiter
for men who have no guts you work your guts out
you work work work
take the money from these evil companies you work
like whores
like mad men
like hell
and no one is dying except for you
you work
until sweat appears
and sits on you
marking your skin
sweat
that your fathers and mothers gave you
who worked like 3-legged dogs
to get up that hill
to get across that canal
to dig for the bone that doesn't exist
that they have made up
so that you keep on working
work work work
work work work
and then you drop down dead
leaving 60-grand of debt behind you

damp in the bathroom
and a sun burning just as bright
as when you were around

controller Donnelley

controller Donnelley tells Harry, his head supervisor
that he is not happy with the way holidays and days off
are being allocated out to the controllers

controller Donnelley tells Harry
that there doesn't seem to be any thinking or planning
behind the way holidays and days off
are allocated
and that this total lack of any strategy
or forethought
causes him to sometimes have to hold on for two or three hours
after his shift
and that when he walks out of the office
to not then think that it is all over for him
because he then has to travel an hour-and-a-half
on the tube
before he gets home
and to not think that even then
it is all over for him
because whenever that happens,
which it seems to be doing
more and more lately,
his wife makes him sleep on the couch
rather in the bed
alongside her

controller Donnelley wants to know what Harry is going to do about it
because if it continues
he thinks his wife will ask him for a divorce
or at least position him in her mind
as a lesser man
than the one she married

Harry, with three divorces behind him
and a fourth wife on his arm
tells controller Donnelley
that he should get himself a good lawyer quick
because wives will inevitably leave you
while you remain in the employment of Phoenix Express
under any capacity
but especially as
a controller

when it's obviously not enough

it obviously wasn't enough for their controllers
to just be there
for 11-hours a day
doing their business
trying somehow to weave together the needs
of the couriers and the clients
placed under intolerable pressures
trying somehow to defuse each bomb placed in their hands
before any of them went off

it obviously wasn't enough for their controllers
to have lost their sense of self, lost their ticking hearts
or to have gone through scores of women
or given up on their dreams, lost a home or two
or that they almost all
had developed a drink and drug need
that most would consider unhealthy

it obviously wasn't enough for their controllers
to sleep the un-sleep
to carve the un-carved
day after day
night after night
or for them to spend all of the hours not doing this job
with it swaying in the mist
on top of the hill at the back of their minds
like a hung corpse

it obviously wasn't even enough that their controllers
had to work one Saturday every month
or that they hadn't fallen in love with anything
in over 8 years
or that they felt that their hands were attached to minds and bodies
that weren't even recognised

because now
they want their controllers to come in every Monday
one-and-a-half unpaid hours before their shifts start
just so they can attend a meeting
to go over all of the issues and matters of contention
of the previous week

how to disappoint almost everybody

we didn't need the supervisor's disgust or hate to know that we weren't
making music
we knew that sat in those big controllers' chairs we were
in the crosshairs of a sniper
completely exposed with our jobs in danger and our lives
sometimes balanced in the wind
we didn't need the reports or feedback from the sales team
telling us that their customers
were unhappy and thinking about moving their accounts
to another company
we didn't need the constant pressure of that
or the couriers getting on the phone telling us that if we didn't make it
happen for them
then they were going to lodge a complaint against us
which would stick like tar poured onto the back of a Spartan's eye
we didn't need the memo we got each month
on the day before we got paid
telling us that our performance related bonuses hadn't been passed again
this month
because we had failed to achieve the 91% performance level that was
required
and we didn't need the HR manager pulling us in
to tell us that we were 'not that far away from a disciplinary'
we didn't need any of that
to tell us that we were failures
we knew that we weren't making music anymore
because we already had women and teenagers at home
who constantly let us know how we had failed them
how disappointed they were
in us not being able to take them away on a summer holiday
once again
just like the last 3 years
or not being able
to put a rock on her finger
despite the years we had been together

sometimes
despite the years of 11-hour shifts you put in
you just have to accept that you will fall short of getting over the line
in almost everything
for almost everyone
disappointing
almost everybody

because he hasn't yet taken her to Rome

he sits on the control point of the busiest courier company in London
controlling 55 couriers
and it is his job to make sure that those 55 couriers earn a living
so that they can pay their rent and for their daughter's ballet lessons
and for their son's after-school clubs
and for their wine and beer
it is his job to make sure that they earn enough
so that they can pay off their debt
their electricity bill
their mobile phone contracts, internet connections
and council tax
it is his job to make these 55 couriers decide to stay with Phoenix Express
rather than leave
to go and work for some other company
along with this
it is also his job to look after accounts
that spend upwards of 22 million pounds a year
making sure that their documents and contracts
arrive on time
so that no shit comes back and splatters itself all over his face
it is his job
to achieve the balance of these 55 couriers needs
along with the needs of these 22 million pounds a year clients
it is his job
to bring all of that together
and those hands of his do it
but all he can think about while he is doing it,
as he explains to us in the pub across the road
after our 55-hour weeks have finished,
is that his woman won't blow him anymore
that she thinks his cock is not good enough for her anymore
as he stitches together these 800 jobs a day
trying to weave together the law firms print designers advertising reps
and big banks' needs
trying to understand the couriers needs also

weaving and sewing it all together
tight enough so that everyone goes home happy
and him
with two bottles of wine under his arm
going home to be told
that his cock is not good enough anymore
because he hasn't yet moved enough mountains far enough for her
because he hasn't yet put a rock on her finger
because he hasn't yet
taken her to Rome

the pouring

people pour into this world unneeded
they pour out of wombs into homes
that don't need them
they pour into schools that don't want them
hold down jobs that don't want them
people pour onto the streets
they head towards supermarkets gymnasiums call centres football matches
they lay in beds inside hospital wards that don't need them
lift up flags whose stars don't need them
pull open doors for people they have fallen in love with
who in 20 years time won't need them
it makes no sense
people bake cakes
for children who will one day not need them
tap away at keypads lift quarter ton engines out of vans just so they can
replace a nut or a bolt
drive
at ridiculous speeds around the streets of London
just to deliver an invite to a black tie event
they sit
on grass and park benches drinking under a sky
that doesn't need them
people fall into the earth that they have sifted through their hands
all of their lives
earth
that doesn't need them grandmothers
dead from cancer
who don't need them mothers
who never needed them
took them aside to tell them they weren't needed
it makes no sense
people pour into this world
like bats and humming birds
like tigers and fists
none of it makes any sense

the man or woman
who writes a poem
scores a symphony
paints
a heart broken open in two over Christ's eyes looking down from
the cross
a black woman's head
stuck on a spike
a sword
pinning everything together between the ground and the stars
for a people
who don't need them
who would rather be
queuing to pay for an avocado
sitting in front of a tele
tapping away at a phone
selling and buying their toes

it makes no sense

people pour into this world unneeded
to gain a hold
to gain a foot
they lie cheat abuse murder
and it is as though it is the most important thing ever
that they succeed

well if this is their success
give me failure
anytime
something
I can understand
lift a drink to

some nights we get it with both barrels

some nights we come out of showers after our 11-hour shifts
wearing our dirty beige dressing gowns
to sit in chairs in front of the tv
with our woman sitting on the couch
flicking through magazines
licking her paws
and her nose in the air

some nights we open up bottles of wine
and pour ourselves glasses full to the brim
placing them down by our naked feet
feeling that we have done just enough
to consider ourselves to be men

'Why did I have to get with a man
who thinks that just doing a job
is enough
to be considered a man?'

we lift the glass beside our useless feet
and sip down the wine
pouring more in from the bottle
every time the glass gets empty

'Why did I have to get with a man
who has no life-plan,
who has no schemes
or big ideas,
who just works and works and works
making money
for other people?'

when the bottle is empty
from all of our sipping
we drag our useless arses up from the chair
and go to the fridge
to open up the other bottle of rose
that we bought
on the journey back from work

'What on earth have I done?
I am going to be here
10 years from now
saying the same shit
and you ain't gonna have done anything more,
or more to the point,
tried
to do anything more
than what you have already done.
You just think that you have
arrived,
don't you!?'

the wine is good
it is making it all feel okay
and if we are lucky
she'll get a call soon from one of her friends
and get a different audience
to listen to her
other than our naked feet
and our useless arses

'Well I'm going to bed
Mr MAN!
I hope you feel all manly
after your job
because I think you're more a slave
than a man.

I actually blame you
for fucking up my life
and I wouldn't let you fuck me
even if you were the last fucking controller
in the whole fucking world!'

she has gone to bed

death must be like this

the silence
the understanding that
your naked feet
and your useless arse
are pointless

it is a beautiful thing
this life love job combination
any more acceptance from her
and we might just start
getting carried away with ourselves
thinking that we have actually
made it

this woman

this woman is there when us controllers come home from work
this woman listens to our moans and gripes about our situations
about how the supervisors in charge of us
are trying to kill us
how they sometimes come out snarling words at us
that pull our egos apart and leave us men feeling like naughty children
this woman
who unpacks the mess we bring home who
keeps the electricity going and the food on the table and
the shoes on our children's feet who
is there when we come back after our 11-hour shifts
when we spit after drinking bottles of wine that no one respects us
this woman making us feel safe and meaningful
putting us back together again after we have split into a million pieces
this woman
who is there all of the goddamn fucking time working
making sure that the kids are fed and get to bed this woman
who has to listen to the drunken mouth of this controller
the bitter heart of this worker
this woman who gave birth to children who puts up with the constant
insecurities
and dramas and wrongs that have been done us this woman
who would much rather be sitting in a deckchair overlooking Lake Garda
with a Campari and soda in her beautiful hand contemplating peace
this woman
who keeps this controller from breaking up into little pieces
who keeps putting this worker back together
day after day, night after night
just so that he can keep going on and on
being a controller feeling almost
like a man
this woman
who is so tired of this controller
that sometimes when he falls asleep
must want to drive a screwdriver through his heart

so that all of the noise will just stop
and the silence
can spread out over her tired limbs
and let her mind start beating again
without having to be a part of all of these controlling things
and all of these supervisor things
ever
again!

in between Stockholm Street and Syndrome Way

Tony is in the pub across the road
drinking tequila and pints of cider
after another one of our 55-hour weeks have finished
and he tells me that sometimes he feels that the hours he spends away
from this job we all despise
are equally unenjoyably

Tony tells me that these hours he spends away from this job
give him time
to churn over in his mind
just exactly how much debt he is in
and how it is a big empty pit that he will never get out of

he tells me that when he gets up on a Saturday morning
these hours he spends away from doing this job
expose the cracks between him and his woman
that the 8 years he's now spent doing these 11-hour days
have driven in

these hours he spends away from doing this job
these weekends where he finds himself walking along the canal
his mind almost always firmly back in the control room
going over all of the politics
again and again
these down hours
which find him unable to sleep
unable to relax
unable to function properly
are equally unenjoyably for him

he tells me after our fifth tequila and sixth pint of cider
that it is strange
because when Monday morning comes around again
purpose begins to prick in him again
and that the walk down to get the bus
to go in to do this job we all despise
is kind of like a walk into meaning for him,
from nothing
into something,
a meaning he cannot explain
but wants me to understand
as we drink our sixth tequila and seventh pint of cider
and look at each other
unable to speak anymore
because we both don't know or understand why
this job we all despise
means so much to us

they own these hands of mine

if I could let these hands go
and see them exactly like they see them
as somehow separate
from the rest of me.

if I could see these hands
just as the things that they pay me for
rather than a part of the rest of me.

it's obvious what they want
because whenever another part of me gets sick
or worn out
so that I can't get these hands into work
they stop my pay
as though the rest of me is going to have to learn,
going to have to suffer,
for stopping these hands from coming in.

if I could only let these hands go
and not see them like I do
as a part of the rest of this thing I call me,
if only I could distinguish the difference between these hands and me...
no, it's no good,
you can't separate the hand from the heart
or the hand from the stomach
or from the eyes, ears, nose
and throat.

if I could detach these hands
from the rest of me,
chuck them on the supervisor's desk
like a pair of old tools,
tell him that he can have them
no questions asked, no lease needed,
if only his pursuit of them doing more and more tasks

faster and faster
stops
so that the rest of me can breathe
and relax,
enjoy the sunshine once in a while,
then I would.

but that's not ever gonna happen
because hands like these
are what keeps their engine's running
while the rest of me
is just so much shit
clogging up their systems.

these hands have made sandcastles too

these hands belong to a controller
and they belong to him
they get this controller into work
and they hold his cup of coffee and feed his bagel into his mouth
these hands adjust the controller's chair
that the previous controller has just left
to the required height and level
so that these hands can do their job
these hands are the only thing that this controller has these hands
have held his woman in his arms as they both together
danced and spun each other around these hands
have sent down jobs to couriers which have made their day
they have also sent down jobs to couriers
which have ruined their day these hands
have held keys to flats that are no longer theirs they have removed
a piece of glass from the screen of a child's eye these hands
have bumped and slapped other hands and held a pen to sign his name
on a marriage certificate and a divorce settlement these hands
have made sandcastles too, they have written out a bet they have
punched and gripped and the fingers that are on these hands
have helped keep this man in a job these hands
have carved out an existence for this man they have held and moulded clay
into a living thing they have made things happen these hands
move across one of their keypads like lightning
letting the fingertips attached to them
drop down on to the keypad
in a such a symphonic and synchronised way
that all of the noise stops for a minute
sometimes even for hours these hands
hold glasses of wine after sunsets and 11-hour shifts
pour them into his eager mouth they are the hands
of a controller
and even though the company that these hands work for
try continually to devise ways to detach these hands from the rest of him
they belong to all of him

and the longer he can keep on believing this
and making it happen
the more chances this controller has
of keeping hold of his job

at the processing plant

there was something going on
with the quality of steel
being used to make the cans
that held in all of this
shit.

more and more consignments were being sent for repair
due to the cans either creasing
or splitting entirely
letting all of its shit out.

sure enough, after tests were carried out
on the quality of steel being brought up to make the cans
it was discovered that the new steel
was made out of a far more inferior steel
than the old steel.

the old steel was tougher
and more predictable,
if you bent it into a shape
and sealed it together with heat
it would stay in that shape
no matter how painful or uncomfortable it got,
but nowadays
with this new steel
nothing stays in any shape for very long,
it just can't seem to take the stresses involved
and creases or splits
whenever it gets too much for it
letting all of its shit out.

but most importantly
the new steel
was found to just contain less steel
than the old steel.

unfortunately
this discovery didn't help
because the supplier of the old steel
had shut down his factory
due to economic reasons
and the new supplier
was unable to produce the quality of steel needed
due to economic reasons.

somehow
they were going to have to find a new way
to contain all of this shit
before every can everywhere
ends up being made of this new steel
which at any unpredictable moment
will just crease or split
letting all of its shit out
causing mayhem
as though it was the most natural thing for a can to do
in the world.

supervisors in fear of Ronnie

the supervisors care about Ronnie
they worry about his mental health
they put him on report
so that they can keep a closer eye on him
their sick little child
their sick little chameleon

the supervisors care about Ronnie
they are concerned that he doesn't always remember
the rules
that he might one day set fire to their office
might put MDMA in their coffee once again
or else climb onto the roof
and refuse to come down

the supervisors care about Ronnie
they call him in for counselling sessions
to discuss how he is getting on
hollowing out his tunnel
plucking the barbed wire from his eyes
finding other crew members
to come with him on his trip to the sun

the supervisors care more than Ronnie's mother cared
more than Ronnie's father cared
more than Ronnie's social worker cared
they care so much
that they have told Ronnie
that soon he might not be able to use their facilities
to play anymore
in case he injures himself
or worse
injures one of them

banned from shooting up nails into a tin ceiling like a cowboy

Ronnie has been banned from going down to the workshop
in his lunch hour
he has been banned from going in there
and picking up the workshops' nail gun and waving it around in the air
shooting nails up into the tin ceiling like a cowboy
banned from picking up those big wide-mouthed spanners in his hands
and chucking them at the walls like a circus knife thrower
banned from laying out 10 tyres side by side on the floor
and running through them
stamping his feet through the centre of each one
like a marine in training
banned from picking up exhaust systems
and holding them in one hand behind his shoulder
pretending to launch them into the air like an Olympic javelin thrower
banned from removing the sump plugs on engines
so that the oil inside them pours out onto the floor
while running around screaming at the top of his voice,
'MAYDAY! MAYDAY!
GET ALL OF THE BIRDS TO SAFETY!
I THINK WE HAVE AN OIL SLICK ON OUR HANDS!'
banned
from taking the air-hose
and placing it in his mouth
before pulling back the silver trigger
that made all of his hair stand up and his eyes to bulge
banned from grabbing 3 or 4 of those mega-sized towel rolls
and going up to the mezzanine floor
before launching them off into the air
so that they streamed out and down onto the workshop floor
all the while screaming 'ARGEN-TINA! ARGEN-TINA!'
banned
from sitting down with the mechanics while they tried to eat their lunch
and telling them that all of these tools and stuff
that they have to play with
makes him feel horny

which was okay
and understandable
but no help to us controllers
who are now going to have to work out a way
to contain all of those fantasies
that run about inside Ronnie's head
while we eat
our lunch

Ronnie and the swans

now that Ronnie has been banned from going down to the workshop
and playing with all of their tools
he has started going over to Sainsbury's to buy a loaf of bread
and then taking that loaf of bread down to the canal
spending his whole lunch break sitting on one of the benches on the
footpath by the side of the canal
tearing off bits of that bread
and feeding it to the swans
and as they all paddle towards the spot Ronnie sits at
Ronnie has started talking to them
asking them questions about life and the Universe
convincing those swans that he means them no harm by smiling and
oohing and ahhhing at them
dropping the torn off bits of bread a little bit closer to him each time
until finally they had to haul their swan arses out of that canal
and come closer and closer to Ronnie if they wanted to get at that bread
as Ronnie kept reeling them in
naming them
talking to them in the sweetest voice he could manage,
'hello, Snowy, you're looking fine today,
I hope nobody ever kills you
and breaks that lovely neck of yours,'
and,'hey,
Flip-Flop,
come to Daddy,
you know Daddy loves you.'
until after a month or so
he had those swans eating bread out of the palm of his hand

4 or 5 swans padding away around Ronnie's feet
as he tore off that bread and fed it to his new babies
with a heart warm enough that it heated up his whole being
'everything,
for once,
is going to be alright,'
Ronnie kept muttering to himself

as the clouds began gathering above his head
and Winter got ready
to make everything dead again

where every day is Winter

Ronnie is having a panic attack
he can't understand why
the swans are suddenly not over by the canal anymore.
'they were there yesterday,
I fed them,
but now they are gone!'

he is hyperventilating
thinks he has done something wrong
or worse
somebody else may have harmed them
and now they will never come back
to eat bread out of the palm of his hand.

the seasons
don't play much of a part in Ronnie's life
up there
every day is Winter.

where have all the rock stars gone

Ronnie used to rock back and forth in his controller's chair
whenever it got busy
he used to grab onto the arms of his chair and throw his head back
onto his neck
so that it pointed perfectly straight up
his eyes drilling straight through that ceiling
and whenever it got too much for him
Ronnie used to suddenly stand up
and snap-shut his knees close enough to his chair so that he banged
that chair hard enough for it to shoot off across the floor
and crash into the wall on the opposite side of the room
as he threw his arms up in the air
and screamed

Ronnie didn't care
about procedures and peace
he only cared about rock stars and his mental health
as he insisted on telling us all
as he remained standing there
having one of his turns
how all of the great rock stars were dead
and we're never coming back
how back in the day
rock stars used to pull vines out of the ground
and twist them around their head
pour
their sick onto the stage
remove
their tongues from their mouths
and wave them about in the air
covering the crowd in spit and words and attitude and dreams

while now
all they do is stand in front of cameras
filming mobile phone commercials
stand in front of lenses with a smile on their face
trying to catch the look that will sell
another pair of sunglasses
another mobile phone contract
as they allow their songs to accompany car insurance adverts
and holiday commercials
while sat away in Hertfordshire homes
drinking smoothies
and posting plates of food up on Instagram

the Universe needs rock stars to keep on expanding Ronnie told us
as he muttered away about their decline
having something to do with his deteriorating mental health

having no rock stars out there
that actually 'rock-n-rolled'
was slowly making him
and the rest of the world
go insane

debt runs like streams of poison through us all

all of the controllers are sitting in a Chinese restaurant on Queensway
attending a bonding dinner arranged by the supervisors

Harry, the head supervisor is here
along with his four henchmen
and they are all trying to explain,
in the hope that us controllers
can buy into the idea
that we are a team,
that the pressures we are under each day
are shared pressures
that they feel as well
and that the bollockings they administer to us
for all of the fuck-ups and all of the late collections we are guilty of
are designed to keep us on our toes
rather than dehumanise and humiliate us

at 10 pm the five of them leave
feeling like they have done their job
while all of us controllers just breathe a sigh of relief
and order more Tiger beers on the tab they have left open for us

at 11 pm the table is literally covered with empty Tiger beer bottles
and the conversation is flowing as Dermot opens up
and tells us all about how much debt he is in

Stevie and Antoine and Marcus tell him not to worry
that they are in debt up to their eyeballs too
and then everyone, to a controller, admits that they are in debt
as well

Dermot, as though he'd found a new idea, asks the waiter
if he can borrow a pen and his order pad
so that he can make a list
of all the controllers
and their debt

we order more Tiger beers and Dermot starts asking each controller
how much debt they are in

Stevie is in debt to his bank for £4,500
from when he took out a loan to go to Thailand
which he is paying back at £150 a month over 3 years
and he also owes his mum £2,000
which he pays back a bit of
whenever he can

Marcus is in debt to two loan companies for £9,000
which is made up of three separate loans
which he took out for reasons he doesn't want to explain
but which the payments combined are £275 a month
and he also has an overdraft of £1,500
which has been maxed out
for the last 18 months
and which eats up his pay-cheque every month

Ronnie is in debt to Mastercard for £18,000
and Visa for £12,000
from when he went through the split with his wife of 12 years
and had to fund payments to her and for this
and for that

Antoine is in debt to his four credit cards for £13,000
and owes his local off-licence
£87.50

Tony is in debt to the loan company he borrowed the money from
to bury his mum
but he is not sure how much it is
apart from it taking £225 a month from his pay

Lucas owes £4,000 to Mastercard
£1,500 to Barclaycard
and £1,800 to Aqua Credit Facilities
which he has accumulated over the years
from just living

Murphy owes his Uncle in Dublin £15,000
from when he relocated from Cork to London
which he pays back at £250 a month
on a pre-arranged family agreement
plus £5,000 to Fish
which gave him a credit card he applied for
one drunken night on the web in his bedsit

Sammy owes £65,000 to 5 different loan companies
which he pays each £25 a month
and then just ignores
the hundreds of letters and daily phone calls he gets
from each of them

I owe £16,000 to Westcott Finance
£22,000 to BDS Collections
and £14,000 to Provident Credit
and I also ignore the letters and daily phone calls
that I get from them each month

debt
it seems
runs like streams of poison through us all
and the numbers and payment dates stuck in their big machines
that eat away at all of our pay packets
and all of our minds
leave us constantly pensive and paranoid
that we will not be able to make anything happen
for us
or our families
ever again

the supervisors were right
we were all part of a team after all
just not the one
they thought

debt-raffle

after our drunken conversation in the Chinese restaurant
about how much debt we were all in
the controllers decided to hold a raffle
to try and raise funds
to help pay off some of that debt.

Marcus procured
a raffle ticket book from Sainsbury's
while Dermot made a list
of the 3 prizes on offer
artfully drawn out on a big pink sheet of A1 card
which he had pinned to the notice board
in the staff's lunch area.

Third Prize: Two weeks washing a controller's underpants.
Second Prize: One week making coffee for a controller,
whenever he asks for it.
First Prize: A night out with a controller of your choice, with sex
compulsory.

it was going to prove a tough sell
but at least all of us controllers
could spend the day of the raffle
in fits of laughter
with something else to occupy our minds other
than the constant pressure placed on us
trying to make sure the client's SLAs were met;
with something else other
than the constant calls from the couriers
bitching that they were being treated unfairly
and not being allowed to earn a living;
with something else other
than the constant fear
that at any minute a supervisor might come out
and rip us apart for fucking up a job;

with something else other
than the constant knowledge,
hung right there in front of our awareness like a death-rattle,
that if everything doesn't go exactly to plan this month,
like the kids suddenly needing an emergency filling
like the boiler suddenly exploding
like the car suddenly breaking down
like a sudden unplanned bill dropping through the letterbox,
then at the end of the month
we might not be able
to pay a bit towards the rent arrears
once again.

that uncontrollable pit of debt

sometimes it just hits you
while you're on the bus
thinking of nothing
staring out at the cranes
or sitting on a train
following a bird flying across the sky
from nowhere
into nothing

it starts at the top of your chest first
from left and right
funnelling in
like a warm liquid
injected into your system
then it quickly gathers at your abdomen doors
you can feel the anticipation
in your guts
the warmness kindling
then
quick as a flash
it burns down those doors
and pours out
all over the walls of your gut
making them tingle and flutter
like when you need to shit
or when you're falling in love
and then the mind picks up on it
identifies the cause
before churning it over and over
each dead-end a padlock snapped shut
each 4,000 foot high wall a chain pulled tighter around your lungs
each flawed escape route a spotlight shone brighter on
the emptiness
the pointlessness
the self
hatred

still
the birds flying across the sky
from nowhere
into nothing
look lovely

a couple of chicken bones in a dog's mouth

if you listened to Ray
the 37 years he's spent in control rooms
has been his saviour

'the only thing that kept me feet on the ground, son,
the only thing that kept me feet on the ground'

the first thing he did every morning
was take the anti-static wipes
and clean down his keypad and monitor
making sure that there was a pen and paper by his side
some coffee, a working phone and a jug of tap water

he delighted in telling the less experienced controllers
stories about the past
'you had to control with your wits back then, lad,
there wasn't any of this computer bullshit,
when couriers got pissed off
they used to come up the office for a straightener,
none of this 'fill out a complaint form please
and we'll get back to you' stuff,
they were there, right in your face,
and you had to just deal with it,
got these scars that way, lad'

the 37 years Ray had spent in a control room
must've had something to do with the two weeks' notice he got
when it became obvious,
when it just couldn't be hidden anymore
that he was never,
not even in another 37 years,
going to grasp the new high-tech operating system
that had recently been installed

and as Ray said
after he told us the news,
'it's funny really,
how 37 years can seem like a couple of chicken bones in a dog's mouth
when placed alongside this technology'

trying to paint the Sistine Chapel over again

the four programmers brought in to develop the
new automated allocating system
have spent the last 18 months shut away in their office writing code
trying to replicate the knowledge of us controllers
in digital format
but for the last 6 weeks
those same developers
have strangely abandoned their office
and come out to sit with us controllers
asking us questions about why we make this decision
and that decision
all the while writing down notes in their little Moleskine books
that will apparently help
hone their monster

we conduct show-and-tell lessons with them
highlighting that our decisions are not always the same
given the same circumstances
because you have to know the abilities of the couriers that are available
as well as the client's expectations
and that that was what us controllers called
a moving target
which we had to hit more often than not
or else lose our jobs

obviously they hadn't listened or quite understood
how complex this controlling lark really is
because if they had
then they wouldn't have signed off
on a new automated allocating system
that goes live next week

which won't be able to paint the Sistine Chapel over again
which won't be able to leap like a Nureyev
which won't be able to carve marble like a Rodin
and which won't be able to see the unseen
or think the unthinkable
quite like us controllers can

but then that isn't the point of the new automated allocating system
the point is to try and force it through
so that directors can sit around tables bigger than the sun
squeezing away at people's lives like they were plastic cups
only to finally be able to reveal to their shareholders
that they might just have found
a new way of doing it
a new way to fly straight through the centre of that sun
while reducing the wage bill of controllers
by at least 10 times 30-grand-a-year
for ever

threatened again

the week before the new automated allocating system was to be introduced
the HR manager called all of us controllers in
one by one
to assure us that our jobs were safe
and to tell us that we needed to embrace this new technology
and see it as a tool
that will help us to do our jobs even more efficiently
than we were currently doing.

unfortunately
they hadn't told the supervisors this
who spent the whole week picking us up on minor issues
before delighting in telling us not to worry
because next week,
after the new automated allocating system has been introduced,
we most probably won't have a job
anyway.

the new automated allocating system

of course it made us all feel uneasy
of course it made us all feel paranoid
and to worry if we were going to keep these jobs
that paid our rent and bills and fed
our families

of course the rumours that its tentacles
armed with a billion sensors
could reach out into everywhere
and suck up all of the information inside our theatre
turning it into little bits
that it could put back together again more beautifully
than any of us controllers could
made us feel threatened

of course the rumours that its artificial brain
which didn't take lunch breaks
or get paid 20 days holiday a year
which didn't drink alcohol or fall sick
or need a woman to hold it in its arms
which didn't have to worry about paying the rent
or the mobile phone contracts
or feed the electricity key
which never forgot a thing
and had the streets and one-way systems of London
and all of the client's service level agreements
programmed into its metallic cortex
made us feel nervous
and inadequate

of course all of that propaganda and rumour
made us controllers confide in each other
and to share with each other
that this must be how those Londoner's must've felt
back in the Blitz

the new automated allocating system
had made the controllers
for the very first time ever
seek ways to hold hands
and think about how best we could all
stick together

finally, in harmony together

Dermot placed his arm around Tony's shoulder
on the walk up the road to catch the bus home
after their shifts had finished

Marcus started speaking
to his fellow controllers across the lunch table
rather than sitting there all aloof and superior

Stevie gave up putting a palmful of salt
into his fellow controller's coffee
whenever they weren't looking

Mikey offered to cover the hour Bart needed off
to go and collect his sick mother
from the hospital

and when controller Donnelly went to buy a drink
he also brought one back for Antoine
his right-hand man

even Ronnie had put down that squeezy ball of his
and that mad stare of his
and started trying to engage with his fellow controllers
pretending as best he could
that he didn't feel like an outsider
who was slowly going mad

this new automated allocating system
that was set to go live next week
was having a strange effect
on these men who normally wouldn't cross the road
to piss on each other
even if they were on fire

not just yet, brothers

when the new automated allocating system went live
us controllers sat back and wondered how long it would be
before we all lost our jobs
but we needn't have worried
because one of the first allocations it gave out
was a Bayswater to Chiswick
to a van with goods on board going to Stratford
which for those who don't know
was like putting two people on a plane leaving Heathrow
with one of them going to New York and the other one going to Moscow;
they were both going to get there
but one of them was going to take a fucking long time.

we should've known though
anything dreamt up by the people who run Phoenix Express
requiring four new members of staff,
costing hundreds of thousands of pounds
and taking nearly 2 years to develop
was bound not to work.

and as Ronnie said one hour into the trial,
'I guess we can all safely load next month's travel money
onto our Oyster cards once again,
brothers.'

anger and agony

the programmers of the new automated allocating system
have finally admitted that it doesn't work
and have advised the board of directors
to withdraw its use
so that they can spend more time tinkering with the logic
that the new automated allocating system uses
to allocate out the jobs

that's more time
getting paid their 70-grand-a-year salaries
trying to come up with an algorithm
that us controllers already have
seared inside our heads

more time
trying to understand the various circumstances
us controllers understand
as easily as we pull on our socks
which we are able to compute
so that we make correct decisions
98 times out of 100
but which the new automated allocating system fluffs
more often than not
sending couriers down jobs they shouldn't get

that's more time
working from home drinking Red Bulls and smoothies
taking breaks to mow the lawn
or skype their programming mates
to discuss other projects
they have going on
as us controllers have to sit in our controllers' chairs for 11 hours a day
on less than half their money
continuing to make decisions
that keeps this 22 million pounds a year company going

talking to couriers and customers about their problems
and instantly solving them
with no time left to pay our rent or our gas bill
with no time left to challenge the county court judgments
or our overdrawn bank charges
with no time left
to consider that if we didn't keep on doing this
then we might even be able to paint a picture
or write a novel
or carve from a piece of steel
a perfect image to represent
our anger and agony

the programmer's return

after 4 months away in the Dordogne
the programmers of the new automated allocating system
have returned.

they look healthy and strong
as they announce that they think they are almost there
transferring the knowledge and guile of us controllers
into their metallic bastard.

their little metallic bastard
who once grown up and able to think properly
will take away all of our jobs,
which if all goes according to plan
will leave this control room completely empty of men,
completely empty except for the purring and whirring
of its gigantic brain
stuffed away inside a little black box
sat on a table in the middle of this room
on a black piece of felt
like a mysterious piece of alien art
which no one is allowed to see
which no one is allowed to understand
and no laughter
anywhere.

the things our hands once stood for

the new automated allocating system will not need hands to press
buttons to send down jobs to couriers
the new automated allocating system will do that automatically
it will not need a man to cover it while it takes a lunch break
a man to sit in its seat while it takes its 20 days paid holiday a year
a man to look after its couriers whenever it calls in sick
because the new automated allocating system
won't ever take lunch breaks
it won't ever need holidays
and it will never ever call in sick
the new automated allocating system won't need the men who for years
have sat in front of their screens
working out which couriers should get which jobs
the men whose hands have helped build this company the same hands
that once helped rivet together the Humber bridge
weld pipes together 2000 feet under the North Sea
that ran gas into villages and cities
that placed a cherry on top of a cake in a baker's
on a high street long ago shut
replaced by Subway McDonalds Starbucks Express chains Pound shops
where bookies and pawn shops sit side by side
and we aren't supposed to get the irony
hands that drop change into the homeless woman's polystyrene cup
because they know that it could be them next
hands that came from hands who once picked up a shovel to dig a
trench
on a battlefield of a war they didn't start
from hands that pickaxed at rock 200 feet under Newcastle freeing the
coal that would power
this progress that these hands are now not a part of
progress that has seen jobs disappear or moved overseas
leaving hands behind
that still need to open a tin of beans throw a steak on a griddle pan
break open an egg
hold a pint of milk stick a fork into sausages

feed them into his mouth
hands that pay rent electricity bills dentist bills council tax insurance
premiums hold their women
at night under skies that break open in thunder
that once hung doors in council flats schools and libraries
welded ships together
replaced the heart or kidney of an 8 year old boy
hands
that soon won't even be needed anymore
whose only use will be
to pick up a pen and write a poem
about the things our hands
once stood for

they can't kill all of what's in us

they cut out our tongues
with hooks and garden shears
with rules and red barbed wire
and now we have no voice anymore;
we still have things to say
and we say them
but nobody can hear us
because they have cut out our tongues.

they removed our hearts
with sniffer dogs and dynamite
with sonars and depth-charges
and now we have no feelings anymore;
we still have women and children
and I'm sure we love them dearly
but we can't feel anything anymore
because they removed our hearts.

they cut out our eyes
with scissors and drops of acid
with scalpels and ice-cream scoops
and now we can't see anymore;
we still look around
with our hands shielding our eyes
but we can't see anything
because they cut out our eyes.

they tried to remove our guts
with pincers and hours
with spells and magic
they tried to remove our guts;
but they couldn't get at all of them,

they left a little bit behind
that fought them back,
hid,
did anything it could
to evade detection,
refusing to give in
or feel sorry for itself.

and that is where we live now,
inside that mighty square-inch of guts
that they couldn't find,
that are all that we have
left.

2 or 3 ounces from nothing

how am I to explain to my fellow controllers that I have used them
and that the million and one ways they decide to rebel against the
system we are a part of and which grinds out the thousands of jobs
we cover each day fire me up with words that I put down
tonight

how am I to explain to my fellow controllers whose jobs walk on the
edges of knives who sit in their controllers' chairs bitching and
moaning each day about the software that can't cope which keeps
stuttering and crashing causing them to miss important double-ups
and eventually the supervisor to come out and lay into them that I
often think while they are being shouted at that this would make
a good poem

how am I to explain to my fellow controllers that this chaos we are
all a part of and which we keep turning up for each day on time for
what now seems like centuries has lead me to dedicate whole nights
into putting it
down

how am I to explain to my fellow controllers that everything we have
gone through has been worth it because it has enabled me to write
these poems that have kept me inches away from insanity and which
have made the glory of the nights worth more than all the horrors
spent doing
this job

how am I to explain to my fellow controllers that the guts we have
developed because of this job have only ever helped a man feel
better and other than what they wanted you
to feel

how am I to explain this to my fellow controllers
but still be able to look them in the eye across the tables we eat our
lunches on
but still be able to drink with them into midnights without them
feeling that they are being
sized up

how am I to explain to my fellow controllers that without them
I am only 2 or 3 ounces
from nothing

Roar!

as we allocated out the thousands of jobs
trying to keep it safe and tidy
so that we could protect our minds and dignity
from the supervisors who would come out
every time they caught us fucking up
and try to strip it all away
by screaming and shouting at us
that we were 'idiots'
and 'fucking morons'
poets are writing about the shadows tulips cast in distilling light

and what help does that give us!

as we spoke to customers
whose jobs hadn't been picked up on time
whose lives now will never be the same
trying to appease them by using our street learned charm
sweet talking them with our treacle tongue's
convincing them that this was a one off
that will most certainly never happen again madam
poets are writing about their sexuality
and how hard it is coming to terms with it

and what help does that give us!

as we tried to manage the couriers needs
tried to convince them that we were not there
just to stitch them up
but were just trying to do our job
because we also had our rent to be paid
and our electricity bill to be paid
and our council tax to pay for
and our county court judgements to pay for
poets are writing about oak trees and how a bowl of fruit
left for a week on one of their 5-grand breakfast tables
gives off a scent that reminds them of their childhood

and what help does that give us!

as we get drunk on wine after our 55-hour weeks
move around our flats naked at 4 am on a Saturday morning
walking into the bedroom
holding our cocks out in front of us like surfboards
for our ladies to hop on
even though she stays half-asleep and screams at us to 'fuck off!'
poets are writing about the smell of their dead father's tweed jackets
and studying what type of poem they should write
if they want that editor
to put them in their magazine

and what good does that do us!

as we sit on toilets drunk
smoking cocaine
letting our heads loll about on our necks in complete happiness
complete uselessness
trying to wipe clean away
the consequences of the debt we are in
the worries of the recent takeover
the recent layoffs
the uncertainty of who will next
be squashed down into a digit
by their crunching of the numbers
and ejected out like a piece of industrial waste
poets are writing gutless poems
about irrelevant subjects
using fake words

and what good does that do us!

every day
when we walk in to do our shifts
put those headphones on
and begin allocating out the work
poets are writing about something

poets are always trying
to write about something

the trouble is
it often doesn't ever mean anything
because none of their lives
are ever falling apart
quite enough to make their poems
ROAR! ROAR! ROAR!

and what good does that do us!

Poets and their Flower Cutters

Mike was reading a magazine on the bus to work and came across the following exchange in a piece titled 'How Poets Share on FB'.

Poet Tom has posted a poem of his onto his FB page and shared it with his 'friends' only. Below is part of the exchange between them regarding that post.

Poet Lucy: Love it Tom! It's super.

Poet Tom: Thank you Lucy, it was lovely to see you again yesterday and to see you perform.

Poet Miles: Tom - you're simply the best - I'm working on a poem called 'All the Daffodils in the World and Me' at the moment – AOW!

Poet Tom: Yes, Miles. *It's good to search inside your soul and reveal to the world your true self.* I hope your poem about the daffodils turns out ok. Cheers, Tom.'

Mike wondered what AOW meant. He had to look it up on Google – found out that it was an acronym for Act Of War which he thought brought Poet Miles' mental health into question if he thought that working on a poem about all the daffodils in the world was an 'Act Of War'.

Mike thought that this was very interesting and wanted to look into it more so he set up a few FB accounts and set about friending poets on FB to see if he could find out what was going on. What follows are a few selective posts that Mike found more interesting than the other ones he came across.

Post 1

Poet Tom has worked 14 days on a poem about smoke. He has called it 'smoke' and posted it up on his FB page clicking 'public' so that everyone can see it.

Poet Lucy: TOM! This is magnificent!

Poet Tom: Thank you Lucy. It took me 14 days to polish and shine.

Poet Dexter: Brilliant Tom. The juxtapositions are confusing at first but read again and again they pull apart layers that normal people don't even know exist!

Poet Tom: Thank you Dexter. You are right. I was worried it wouldn't be understood by normal people at first but then as soon as I reminded myself that poetry isn't for normal people it all fell into place.

Poet Lance: Well done, Tom. Stupendous cadences.

Poet Tom: Thank you Lance. It took me 14 days to find them. The one that ends verse 4 came to me while I was eating a bowl of quinoa and cherries.

Poet Lance: Quinoa and cherries? I'll have to try that!

Poet Annabel: Oh Tom, you've gone and done it again – just where does it all come from?

Poet Tom: Well, I'm not quite sure Annabel, it did take 14 days for it to surface so I can only assume that it comes from somewhere deep inside me.

Mike From Bermondsey: The last time I checked Tom, smoke came out of a poet's arse.

BLOCK MIKE.

Post 2

Poet Lance has made a cake with his adopted child Symphony. The two of them have spent the whole of a Saturday afternoon mixing and baking a cake so that when Poet Lance's partner, Poet Miles, comes home from a performance they can surprise him. That afternoon, and Poet Miles' face when little Symphony presented him with the cake, meant so much to Poet Lance that he has written a poem about it which he has posted up on his FB page.

Poet Lucy: Ahhhhh, Lance, that is so touching.

Poet Lance: Thank you Lucy. You should've seen Miles' face.

Poet Crikey-Ellis: Wonderful Lance. Those who think two men can't create a loving inspiring home life for a little girl are going to be shocked by this.

Poet Lance: thank you 'through tears'

Poet Tilly: Lance, just superb! Need to send that one off – I know an editor who is looking for poems for his next edition that use the metaphor of cooking and how it brings children and families closer together to show how the destruction of the working class family unit is pure fantasy perpetuated by the Nazis in the media.

Poet Lance: Do you think so Tilly? I thought it held a deeper meaning other than just the baking of a cake when I was writing it.

Poet Tilly: Defo Lance. So textualised. It reminds me of Larkin in his prime.

Poet Lance: Thank you Tilly. I do see what you mean. PM me the editors details over and I'll send it off to him.

Poet Tom: I've just recently finished a poem about cooking the last white tiger on earth and how from destruction and extinction can rise a most uplifting unity. Do you think your editor would be interested in that, Tilly?

Poet Crikey-Ellis: That sounds amazing Tom.

Poet Tilly: Sounds right up his street Tom.

Poet Tom: It is amazing Crikey-Ellis, even though I say so myself.

Poet Lance: Yes, Tom. Sounds like a poet's poem. But then you've always tried to be one of them haven't you. Always tried to show how you are able to dive deeper soar higher!

Poet Tom: Thank you Lance. Though I feel I should be saying 'oouch'. Did Symphony like the collection of dead hornets I brought her back from Marrakesh by the way?

Poet Lance: Fuck you Tom! You bitch! You've never even been to Marrakesh! Tilly, if you message Tom those editor's details I won't invite you to Symphonies art exhibition at the prep!

and so the poet's world spins
as the cakes get baked
and no white tigers roar upon the earth anymore, Mike thought,
while watching everything going on
out of the eyes of one of his FB accounts.

Post 3

Poet Tom hasn't written a poem for over 14 minutes. He is pacing up and down his study unable to work out what is going on. Every time he gets a thread of a line inside his head he goes to his Vivio laptop and before he can get it down it's gone. This has never happened to Tom before. He decides to post up on his FB page a cryptic message to all of his friends about his predicament.

Poet Tom: the seas are liquid steam but the desert's are upon me.

Poet Lucy: That's cryptic Tom. Are you working on a poem?

Poet Tom: I wish Lucy. It was just a thought I had.

Poet Miles: All poems begin as thoughts Tom. It's what happens next that makes the magic.

Poet Dexter: So are you saying, Miles, that poets are like magicians?

Poet Tilly: Like?

Poet Moonbeam: I like to think that poems are made of fairy dust that gets blown down to Earth on the solar wind...

Poet Dexter: Okay, Tilly...ARE magicians.

Poet Newton: Magicians make me laugh...poetry makes me think, at a kind of molecular level.

Poet Moonbeam: ...and that poets are somehow the Universe's hoovers.

Poet Miles: So, Moonbeam, are you saying poems are the emptying out of an old hoover bag?

Poet Newton: More like the oscillation of a giant dynamo centred inside a star that IS ME!

Poet Anouska: I think Magician's is a great collective for us all. We make the magic happen.

Poet Tom: I think my wand is broken.

Poet Tilly: Oh no Tom...

Poet Miles: OMG

Poet Dexter: Are you ok mate?

Poet Newton: OMFG

Poet Moonbeam: The Universe is a lesser place Tom. Get fixed soon xxx

Poet Lance: Good. LOL.

Post 4

Poet Tilly has just returned from visiting the Why Oh Why poetry festival in Little Munchkins, Somerset. She has been enthused by the whole vibe and the poets she has got to meet and chat with over the last 4 days have made her a little hyper. Though, unusually for Tilly, she hasn't written a poem about it yet, she nevertheless has posted the following up on her FB page.

Poet Tilly: Just returned from Why Oh Why. Absolutely super time. Got to meet so many fantastic poets and there were other people there too, buying books, I think. The vibe was just so inspirational. I think I have enough to write about for a whole year!

Poet Tom: Sounds excellent Tilly. Did you see my book on any of the stalls?

Poet Tilly: Yes Tom, I saw your book!

Poet Miles: I heard Panda Bear Braithwaite read there this year. Did you catch her?

Poet Tilly: She did. I sooooooo much wanted to see her read but the tickets to see her were sold out for like months before. I did see her though...in between readings. What a truly inspirational woman she is.

Poet Tom: they asked me to come down and read this year but I couldn't on account of mother.

Poet Miles: Awwww. Hope she's getting better Tom.

Poet Tom: Not really Miles. She just sits in her armchair as I feed her fingers of bread dipped in warm milk.

Poet Lucy: She's lucky to have a son like you Tom. Not many men of 36 would still be living at home with his mummy. It must hold you back so much.

Poet Tom: Well yes Lucy, it does a bit. I did nearly leave once, when I was 28, but mother made such a scene and then what with the stroke I sort of am still here.

Poet Lance: Mucho Proseco I bet Tills?

Poet Tilly: I'd say Lance. Every time I fart bubbles come out of my arse!

Poet Lance: Haw Haw! Till's? LOL

Poet Crikey-Ellis: LOL

Poet Moonbeam: LOL

Poet Tilly: I'll PM you something later Lance. Let me know what you think.

Poet Lance: Ok Tills

Poet Tom: sometimes I want to just put a pillow over her face so it can all be over...

Post 5

PM post between Poet Tilly and Poet Lance.

Poet Tilly: I slept with Edward Howls!!!!

Poet Lance: OMG OMG OMG NO WAY!!! How? When? Where?

Poet Tilly: At Why Oh Why. He was coming out of Panda Bear Braithwaite's reading and we bumped into each other.

Poet Lance: bumped into each other? you mean more like you saw him and then rammed him you mean!!

Poet Tilly: LOL

Poet Lance: So? What did he do? Where did you do it? Was he good?

Poet Tilly: Lance, it was amazing. Being with him was just like being inside one of his poems. He was so gentle but rough at the same time. Like he was lambing or holding a kitten's head in a barrel of water. Every word he uttered was like a shell coming out of the barrel of his throat.

Poet Lance: they generally are Tills

Poet Tilly: What?

Poet Lance: words / they generally do come out of the barrel of a throat.

Poet Tilly: But his words were special Lance. They literally put a spell on me.

Poet Lance: So what happened next?

Poet Tilly: We sat under a willow tree and talked, he read some of his poems to me, we grabbed a bottle of Prosecco, we ended up back at my B&B together.

Poet Lance: And?

Poet Tilly: He literally riveted me to the bed – hands feet arms legs head tongue vagina – he took it all in his big poet hands and made me...you know...it was amazing.

Poet Lance: And was he a big poet?

Poet Tilly: Not so much a big poet, more a DONKEY poet!! LOL

Poet Lance: OMFG! So happy for you Tills, you deserve a bit of success.

Poet Tilly: Thank you Lance. I left him my number and just waiting now I guess for him to call or text.

Poet Lance: why don't you text him?

Poet Tilly: He didn't give me his number.

Poet Lance: Oh Tilly...?

Post 6

The lead singer of Icelandic folk band Kunda Ka-Ka has committed suicide using a frozen fish. The details are unclear at the moment but Poet Tom thinks that if he posts this up on his FB page it will be obscure and mysterious enough to help perpetuate the obscure and mysterious image he tries to perpetuate.

Poet Tom: Sad day. A few hours ago Morton Freeze of Icelandic folk band Kunda Ka-Ka committed suicide at the tender age of just 27. Not only is it a tragic loss for Icelandic folk music but a tragic loss for world music as a whole.

Poet Miles: is he the guy who played at the Berlin Wall with Sinead O'Connor?

Poet Tom: Not that I recall Miles but he did front the Ka-Ka's when they played on the Slippery Glacier stage at Mortaledbury. Superb gig.

Poet Moonbeam: The Universe is a lesser place.

Poet Lucy: Have you written a poem about it yet Tom.

Poet Tom: As a matter of fact Lucy, I have.

Poet Lucy: I bet it's super. share share share

Poet Miles: Yes Tom, share – NOW!

Poet Tom: Ok guys, pinging it over to you now. I've written it mainly in English but with every 4th word in Hebrew and the last word of each stanza in Icelandic in memory of Morton. Let's see who can work that out !?!? I had the Autumn edition of My Lonely Lymph Gland in mind. You know how dark that editor is. Let me know if you think he will like it or not. If not, any other editor's you think would consider publishing it – with a tweak or two of course, or even a whole revamp, if you think that is necessary.

Post 7

Poet Lucy has just got home from attending an open mic event at the Gob And Guts in Eltham High Street. She is shaking, crying, beside herself with shock. Every time she sits down in her comfortable armchair she soon has to jump up again. She just can't quieten what has been opened up inside her.
Finally she logs onto her FB page and begins to calm down.

Poet Lucy: Awful night at an open mic event in Eltham tonight. Quite literally, awful!

Poet Tilly: Awww. What happened Luce?

Poet Lucy: it was fine at first Tilly, though some of the people were a little uncouth they were talkative, pleasant. One of them even bought me a drink, though it did take me 30 minutes to get it across to the barmaid what an Aperol Spritzer actually was. Not sure it was even Aperol in there either. One of them kept asking me 'ow's that Irn Brew taste with the fizzy water love?' Haven't a clue what he meant or what Irn Brew stands for. I'm guessing it's an acronym, is it?

Poet Miles: Eltham? What the hell was you doing in Eltham?

Poet Tom: No. I think it's a fizzy drink that they sell in Lidl's.

Poet Lucy: It was an organised event Miles. Open mic. All poets, MC's and Roadmen welcome it said. I thought it'd be good. The roadmen that tarmaced the road behind the conservatory the other week were charming.

Poet Newton: Nothing is as it seems.

Poet Tilly: So what happened then?

Poet Lucy: it kept getting later and later. Everyone was drunk and smoking marijuana. Finally, at about 10 o'clock I was invited to read first. God...I don't want to go into it...just to say, I am super stressed.

Poet Tom: what poem did you read?

Poet Lucy: Seven Kittens Standing Under The Open Sky.

Poet Annabel: I love that poem. Especially the bit about the kittens confusion when they realise that their mother has vanished. So urban. Brilliant metaphor dealing with what working to lower class families have to deal with.

Poet Moonbeam: The Universe is a better place for that poem.

Poet Lance: Yes, great choice of poem Lucy. The bit where the kittens in their confusion all start speaking in different languages to each other is a spectacular piece of writing. I bet it had them all clapping away in confusion?

Poet Lucy: it didn't go down well Lance. None of it did. There was only one language they all new and I have never ever been taught it

Poet Anabel: I read somewhere that language one can't understand is either of alien origin or something they call 'street'. It's awful and rather scary.

Poet Miles: Yes, I've heard of that before. My grammar teach taught me that they concocted it up to make them feel all superior and different to people like us.

Poet Moonbeam: all streets lead to the centre of the sun.

Poet Crikey-Ellis: I've just looked up Roadman on the internet. Nothing about tarmac in there at all. I think you might have made a mistake Lucy.

Poet Lucy: I think so to Crikey-Ellis. Never again though.

Poet Tom: Did you see anyone there with my book Lucy?

Post 8

Poet Lance has just opened up an email from an editor who liked a poem Lance sent him about the shoes of his dead father and has suggested to Lance that he would be willing to publish a pamphlet of poems based around the idea of a dead father's clothes and shoes and what not. There is a deadline though of December 1st. It is only early June but Lance is getting all stressed about it. Since opening the letter Lance has drunk 6 espressos from his Nespresso machine, smoked 18 cigarettes, watched 2 hours of Loose Women and eaten 4 figs – but still he can't pull himself together. He decides he needs to share this stressful moment with his friends on FB.

Poet Lance: I've got a deadline coming up and I've only got 6 months left !!!

Poet Tom: Fucking hell Lance. You aren't ever going to make it.

Poet Lance: Thanks for your support Tom. This is fucking up-there-serious so don't muck around with me OKAY!!!

Poet Moonbeam: Relax. Take a deep breath. Let the Universe guide your pen.

Poet Lance: NOT HELPING MOONBEAM!

Poet Dexter: I find that deadlines don't help. They constrict the flow and energy that's needed if you want to be a great writer.

Poet Lance: I know Dexter. I'm totally fucking stressed.

Poet Lucy: Calm down Lance. How many poems do you need to edit?

Poet Lance: EDIT? I HAVENT EVEN FUCKING WRITTEN THEM YET!

Poet Tom: LOL

Poet Lucy: Oh. How many poems do you need to write then?

Poet Lance: I don't know. I've got 1 done so another 19 I guess.

Poet Lucy: Oh. And when is the deadline?

Poet Lance: December 1st

Poet Tom: That's 6 months away Lucy btw.

Poet Lance: Fuck off Tom.

Poet Lucy: It'll be ok Lance. 6 months is a long time.

Poet Lance: it isn't Lucy. 6 months is like tomorrow in the poetry world. Do you know how long it takes a poet even to get an idea! And then there's all of the fucking words and stuff to come up with. I don't think I'll be able to do it.

Poet Tom: Nor me. LOL.

Poet Moonbeam: The Universe will show you a way.

Poet Lance: are you fucking with me moonbeam!?

Poet Tilly: you can do it Lance!

Poet Lance: I can't. I have no ideas.

Poet Moonbeam: that was rude Lance. I curse you with Saturn's eyes!

Poet Lance: I just want to kill myself. Why the fuck did I send that poem off and get myself into this mess in the first place.

Poet Tom: Go on Lance. I dare you to do it.

Poet Lance: What? I can't do anything

Poet Tom: kill yourself.

Poet Lucy: TOM!

Poet Lance: you're a cunt Tom

Poet Lance: I'm doing it !!!!!!!!!!!!!!!!

Poet Lucy: Lance?

Poet Miles: Lance - don't be stupid !!

Poet Tilly: Lance?

Poet Tom: Fuck ME, he might've done it, I didn't mean it

Poet Moonbeam: the Universe is a much better place

Post 9

Poet Crikey-Ellis has shared a link with his friends on his FB page about an article in an online magazine called *Poets and their Flower Cutters*. It is about the link between the progress humanity has made over the last 20 years and the rising number of poets who are writing totally brilliant poems. Apparently the totally brilliant poems help to galvanise everything and move things forwards, or backwards, or whatever the case may be. But because *Poets and their Flower Cutters* is a satirical magazine they have replaced the words 'brilliant poems' with the word 'bollocks'.

Poet Crikey-Ellis: Thought this was interesting. Thoughts anybody?

Poet Dexter: Great angle Crikey-Ellis. Love the semantic camouflage. Makes you think doesn't it...without our 'bollocks' we might not be where we are today.

Poet Annabel: Well, being a lady, I haven't got any bollocks as such, but I have been told that my pamphlet is full of 'bollocks', so I do get it.

Poet Lance: Miles likes to look at my 'bollocks' every night just before he goes to sleep.

Poet Moonbeam: My father, Sun Ray The Lightbringer, who was a fabulously gifted and confusing poet as you all know, used to show me his 'bollocks'every morning at the breakfast table when I was growing up. I have always thought that seeing those 'bollocks' at such an early age helped me to understand the weird relationship this world has with 'bollocks'.

Poet Newton: This article is onto something. Progress has been proved time and time again to be linked to 'bollocks'.

Poet Dexter: So if I am getting this right, this article is suggesting that if it wasn't for our 'bollocks', then there wouldn't be Brexit, a social housing crisis, worldwide poverty and institutionalised racism?

Poet Miles: Lance has a book full of 'bollocks' that Symphony shows to her girlfriends when they come over for a sleepover. I don't think any of them understand them but I do think it is great for young girls to be exposed to 'bollocks' at an early age.

Poet Crikey-Ellis: I think more to the point Dexter is if your 'bollocks' swayed like a ten-ton bell against all of that then there might have been the chance that all, or some of that, might not have happened. But because your 'bollocks' don't sway one way or the other, even in a hurricane, then everything has just been allowed to happen.

Poet Tilly: I haven't told you all about this before but I once had one of Edward Howl's 'bollocks' in my hand as he tore another one off and fed it into my mouth.

Poet Tom: This article sounds eminently plausible. All of my poems are 'bollocks'.

Poet Crikey-Ellis: Thank you everyone. Much to think about. But one thing I think we all agree upon, a poet's 'bollocks' can, and do sometimes, change everything.

as the poets write about the smell of their dead fathers' tweed jackets

a crust of dry bread has become the dream of millions
running water and one bar of electric heat
amenities out of reach for a quarter of the globe
as CEOs stand in their kitchens
warming their feet on underground heated slate tiles
while peeling an avocado
slate
ripped from the earth by people whose hands
have to squeeze the last drop of milk from a dead breast
wring a sleeping bag dry
so they can sleep at night without freezing their guts
people who have jobs but still have to queue in food banks just to feed
their families
as their Prime Ministers and Presidents talk about nuclear wars
destroy
whole communities with an idea they had while playing a round of golf
people who once worked on a farm or in a call centre
or under the ground
who now have no jobs because of an agreement
signed on a jet 30,000 feet above the clouds
people who are moved on from country to country
unwanted
who have to live in makeshift camps for years
just because their God lost an election
and had His fingertips replaced on the trigger of a gun
people who can't clothe or take their children on a holiday anymore
because the price of oil drained from the ground 5000 miles away shot up
into the sky
and closed all of their factories
people who once worked in industries long ago shut by progress
who once used their hands to rivet together ships
haul a piece of steel out of a blast furnace
replace the heart of a 12 year old girl hand over a cup of tea to a miner
squeeze tomato ketchup into a factory worker's bacon sandwich

who now sit at home with nothing to do
using those same hands to put together 1000 piece jigsaw puzzles
or knit hats for their grandchildren who will grow up to be a
number
on a list of numbers who don't have any jobs

as the poets write about the smell of their dead fathers' tweed jackets
are Forwarded £5,000 for a poem about the opening of a wardrobe
have enough time on their hands
to stand in front of mirrors
contemplating whether they exist or not
and books about wizards and bondage
sell millions

when a saxophone or a pen were the only weapons we needed

I remember the days before we were owned by big corporations
when controllers used to come into work hungover from the night before
after they had drunk wine until they couldn't stand up or put their arms
around their woman
and whisper into her ear that they still loved her those days
when they still knew that they would keep their jobs
and get another chance
to make things right I remember
the days when controllers used to be allowed to take random breaks
and go outside to smoke a cigarette looking up at the sky
while talking to their colleagues about politics and Prime Ministers
thinking that there still was a chance to save the homeless man sat on the
corner of Edgware Rd
holding his hands out for change as they passed him by
on the way to work
to save
the alcoholic woman in the flat next door
who kept them awake all night playing Nina Simone on her stereo
at full blast when they still thought
that they could save the NHS and the press and the education system
when they could
still lay out on a Saturday afternoon after 5 days of 11-hour shifts
sipping at a cold beer on grass greener than emeralds under trees
that talked to each other in the wind
waiting for the stars to shine in the night sky like bonfires of hope
without insecurity and fear
crawling all over their bodies like ants I remember
those days when we didn't have to take random breathalyser tests
before we started our 11-hour shifts
and the supervisor sending us home if we failed when there wasn't
a Tesco Express on every street and communities would gather
outside corner shops to talk about their daughters and sons
who were leaving home and starting their first job in the bright
enchanted world I remember

the days before everything became a commodity
before jobs became mere numbers that could be fed into a machine
only to not come out the other side where land
once propped up youth clubs in which teenagers could get excited about
their first kiss where
land held up libraries where men and women could get away
from the cold
and come across the words of Blake or Bukowski our land
that has now been sold off to entrepreneurs and corporations
where blocks of luxury flats glisten in the sun, stars
hang in the night sky over
too far away now
for any of their hope to reach us
when footballers didn't earn more in a second
than controllers nurses firemen teachers call centre operators
and factory workers earn
in a week
where a pub landlord would welcome in a group of men
rather than telling their staff to keep an eye on them where
you could walk anywhere even into the sun
and pull out a saxophone or a pen
only to sing
that everyone still had a chance
and people would actually believe it

learning curve

the new supervisor is telling me
that I should put a house docket through
to pay Delta Six-Six his £80
for the day he had off last Thursday
when he had to take his kid to the hospital

I ask the new supervisor if he is sure
because I don't want this coming back on me
and me getting my arse chewed or put on report

the new supervisor tells me
that from what he can see
Delta Six-Six hasn't had a day off in over 6 weeks
so not paying him for last Thursday wouldn't be fair
or send out the right message
if we want to keep Delta Six-Six motivated
to continue working for Phoenix Express

I ask the new supervisor if he has discussed this
with the old supervisors
which he hasn't
and which explains everything
because when the old supervisors get to hear about this
they will pull the new supervisor aside
and tell him that if he wants to make a career
out of this supervising lark
then he'd better learn quick
that you never ever give anything back
or make a decision
that one of the directors hasn't ratified in the first place

there are reasons
why no one feels a part of anything
around here

this supervisor racket

at our yearly reviews
we listen intently to the HR manager ask us questions
about our situation
and whether or not we think we have
made any progress this year

we tell her that we have
and that the longer we spend in the employment of Phoenix Express
the more we understand what our company
is trying to achieve
and that in a few more years
we hope that we will have come on enough
to be considered
for promotion into a supervisor

the HR manager then explains to us
what a supervisor's role means
she tells us that supervisors have to maintain
a constant positive attitude
even when things seem to be going wrong
left, right and centre
and that not only do the customer's problems need resolving
but also the staff need to be included in the resolution
so that hopefully
the service failure will not repeat itself

it is a very tough ask the HR manager tells us
and that is why the supervisor title
carries with it such a high reward

we already know how much the supervisors are paid
because after a service failure
the supervisors like to pull us controllers
in front of everyone
and rip our fucking heads off
before detailing out
in slow children's tv-language
the way we should have gone about things
so that the fuck-up the controller was guilty of
wouldn't have happened
in the first place
before finishing off
by telling us controllers
'and that's why
I get paid 20-grand-a-year more than you
you muppet'

given the chance
we knew that we would make good supervisors
being included in so many resolutions to service failures
had given us a telling insight
into their art
and, it seems
a greater understanding than most
of how much these guys
were really worth

you can't work at a control point for 11 hours a day...

you can't work at a control point for 11 hours a day and not ask why
so much importance is placed on the delivery of a document
when a woman in the room next door
has to visit a food bank every other night
to beg for a bag of pasta
because her 40 hour a week telephonist job
doesn't provide her with enough money
to feed her children

you can't work at a control point for 11 hours a day
and not learn sympathy
for the man with only one leg
who every day sits propped up against the phone box on Edgware Road
holding his hands out for change
as you pass him by on the way to your job

you can't work at a control point for 11 hours a day
and not learn humility
for the couriers who have to sit on their bikes
and drive around London
only to earn the same money as us controllers earn
in half the time it takes them to do that job

you can't work at a control point for 11 hours a day
and not go home to a flat at night
with wine, heat and hot water
and not wonder
that despite all the probes we have sent into space
and all the hands and feet we have put on the moon
and all the rivers and seas we have held back
and all the almost dead species we have saved
why we still haven't yet managed
to produce a system
in which every man woman and child
has access

to a roof over their heads

you can't work at a control point for 11 hours a day and not feel privileged
not feel lucky
that at least you have avoided the streets
the jails
and the institutions
and that compared to some
everything you have had to put up with
has been easy

you can't work at a control point for 11 hours a day
and not learn to see the world like this
or if you can
then you are most probably not a controller anymore
but a supervisor

alive and on fire

the gods and Thatcher and women and kids and the rent and the bills
had all done their best
to suck the life and fire
out of us
but none of them were anywhere near as effective
as supervisor Glyn

whenever one of us ran late enough on a job
to cause the client to get on the phone
and scream at him
he'd come storming out of his office
straight up to the offending controller
and begin hollering at him

for a full minute or so
he'd just stand there in front of you
screaming obscenities
making sure that everyone else
heard what a useless fuck this
and what a useless cunt that
you were

it was no good trying to act
as though you didn't care
or give a damn
because the longer you pretended that
the more he'd try to rip you apart

you had two choices
either you got up and walked out
or you just fronted it
hoping that it would stop
before it became impossible
for you not to break down
or else throw a fist
into his mouth

I guess some of us
just needed those damn £400-per-week controlling jobs
a bit more than we needed to feel alive
or on fire

supervisor Glyn

when you think about the amount of flesh and blood
and the amount of smiles and souls
he took apart over the years
inside that control room
all those trainee controllers
he knew he'd never let make it
the way he used them
to promote his authority
by getting them to stand up inside that control room
in front of everyone
rather than taking them aside
and having a quite word with them
before booming his big sergeant-major voice at them
that made them tremble and crack
just so that everyone could see
how tough he was
and how he shouldn't be
fucked with
the way he lured out all those family and mortgage controllers
who were good at their jobs
and there for the duration
but who once said the wrong thing
in front of the wrong people
the way he never forgot
that
and set about slowly crushing them
insisting they cover Sunday or midweek night-shifts
or making a big scene of having to pull them off the box
on a busy Friday afternoon
undermining any standing they had
inside that control room
knowing that it would only be a matter of time
before they would snap
and do something unacceptable
like punching him full in the face

or screaming at him that he was a cunt
so he could then
justify sacking them

when you think about all of that flesh and blood
and all of those smiles and souls
he took apart over the years inside that control room
just because he was allowed
to feel that he could

not helping Glyn

supervisor Glyn was hot blooded
and it was a given that you shouldn't cross him
if you wanted to keep hold of your controlling job

he had the responsibility of making sure
that we had enough cover
for nights and for weekends
which Phoenix Express paid a £30 docket for
plus time-and-a-half for any job done

supervisor Glyn used to come out into the control room every Friday
with his clipboard and pen held out in front of him
demanding that us controllers
call out the shifts he needed to fill
over the radio

as a supervisor
Glyn had a lot to protect
but even more to lose
if what he was responsible for
didn't run smoothly
so the longer it took him to fill out those forms,
cover all of those shifts,
the closer he got to losing everything
and the more agitated and aggressive he got
which sometimes caused him to run up and down the control room
threatening us controllers with our jobs
if we didn't find couriers to cover the shifts he had left
right
now!

we all, of course, understood the pressure that supervisor Glyn was under
and we all, of course, called furiously into our mics
for volunteers to work nights and weekends
as we all, of course, neglected
to actually press our foot down on the pedal
so that the couriers out there
couldn't actually here us

it was traumatic
having our livelihoods threatened like that
but nowhere near as traumatic as it was for Glyn
hopefully

wrong seat, brother

if supervisor Glyn walks out one more time
to tell everyone that he lived in Nigeria for 4 years
followed by an anecdote about bush meat
that is so blatantly designed just to impress us

if he for one minute thinks
that telling us controllers that his father was a chief executive for Unilever
which caused him to have to move around the globe
from school to school all through his childhood
is going to light a kernel of sorrow in us for him

if he thinks for one nanosecond
that the stories he tells us
about the weekends he spends up at his wife's family cottage
in the Cotswolds
or about his wife's brother
landing a six-figure-job with Morgan Stanley
is in any way going to impress us

if he thinks that coming out into our control room
and telling us these stories about his life
is in anyway going to help endear him to us
help us controllers forget
the brutal comments he's chucked at us over the years
the searing threats he's levelled at us before
about taking away our jobs
because he considers us 'idiots'
and no more worthy than 'cockroaches'

if he thinks that because he shares with us his life's intimacies
then we will think any less
of the snide back-stabbing politics
we know he has been guilty of
which have ruined some controllers and their families
lives before

if he thinks for one minute
that him coming out and telling us controllers
about how his brother died in a road traffic accident in Switzerland
when he was only 13
with him sat next to him in the back seat
escaping totally unhurt
how he has trouble now dealing with the guilt
sometimes wishing that he had been sat in that seat
instead of his brother
which keeps him unable to sleep some nights
is going to stop us controllers
from continuing to hate him
then he is mistaken

because the Earth would be a far better place
and the trees would grow more stronger
and the flowers would grow more brighter
if only we'd all got our wish
and he'd been sitting in that seat
instead of his brother

blood surrounding his boots

the police were called in today
because Bravo Four-Nine was in the office
demanding his £500 5-day-guarantee payment
even though he'd only worked 3-days

he stood there in front of supervisor Glyn
and after listening to him
explain why he wasn't going to be getting any more money
Bravo Four-Nine started shouting and swearing at him
before suddenly picking up his helmet and swinging it
straight into the side of supervisor Glyn's head

supervisor Glyn fell down
and didn't move
as Bravo Four-Nine, with his helmet in his hand
stood over him
screaming and swearing at him
smashing it more into him
as supervisor Glyn's blood
started to surround his boots

two other supervisors suddenly appeared
and grabbed Bravo Four-Nine in a headlock
before bundling him out of the office
onto the pavement outside

the police were called
as 15 controllers and right-hand men watched on,
not one of us feeling like we should move
or lift a finger
to help,
because that supervisor now laying on the floor
with blood leaking from his head
had once told every last one of us
that we were no more than cockroaches,

that we should carry on allocating out work
and not stop even if there was a nuclear war,
even if there was a death in our families,
because that was all we were good for
and paid for
as we all
for the first time ever
decided to ignore a ruckus unfolding inside the office
and carried on allocating out the jobs
as though nothing else mattered
just how supervisor Glyn
liked

five members of staff

after the recent culling of staff
due to a sudden drop in revenue from the loss of a few big accounts
the Board of Directors asked the supervisors to report
on why the service levels have gone down
from 89% to 83%

the supervisors are unsure what to do
as though it was the Board of Directors who ultimately made the decision
on who had to go
it was the supervisors who allowed it to happen
without saying anything about the potential threat to the service levels
for fear of being marked out
as a troublemaker

and now we are here
and the supervisors will not have the guts to tell to the Board of Directors
that the drop in service levels is because we have five less staff now
it will be far easier for them to lay the blame at the controllers who are left
who they will say have underperformed
because then the directors will be able to shake free their dragon wings
and breathe fire down onto the boardroom table
before advising HR to put the controllers left
under 'a little bit of pressure'
and tut-tutting at the supervisors
for letting this happen
while they go about
fixing it

which, by the way
will require five new members of staff

smashing through the doors of a heart

the heart attack that Phil had
while sat at his control point trying to look after 45 couriers and 600 jobs
which made him sit up rigid as a cadaver
before letting out a last sucked in gasp of air
that echoed out of his lungs like a big old creaky oak door
opening for the first time in centuries
startling the rest of us controllers to look over at Phil
only to see him fall off the side of his chair
and smack his head on the edge of his desk
pulling the mouse that his hand had frozen around
with him onto the floor
was the same heart attack
that Peter our old van controller had 8 years ago
in this very same room

the heart attack that caused Phil
to lay on the control room floor
with blood leaking from the bridge of his nose
holding himself so tight that it looked like he was cuddling something
as his fellow controllers gathered around him calling for somebody to
'call an ambulance'
or to 'get him on his side' or 'keep him warm'
only for him to suddenly stop spasming
and relax
so that his hand released the mouse and his head fell to one side
with one eye open and one eye closed
was the same heart attack that Flanagan
petrified of having
left us for
to go and work for 10-grand-a-year less
in a little mini cab office
attached to the side
of Surbiton station

the heart attack that Phil had

after putting in 12-years of 11-hour shifts without one day off sick
forgoing his lunch hours whenever the control room had been left short
of controllers
covering Saturday shifts at a last-minutes notice
having his concerns ignored about more and more couriers being placed
on his circuit
which he had to look after and make sure earned a living
constantly being pulled up or shouted at by supervisors who never once
pulled Phil into their office
to tell him that he was doing a good job
is the same heart attack that hides in every control room
on every factory shop floor
or wherever else there are supervisors wanting more out of a man
even though he has given his all

the same heart attack
that hangs onto the walls of every controllers' arteries
waiting for the right combination
the correct scent to pass by its nostrils
before unhooking itself
and letting itself hurtle through the blood
before reaching maximum velocity
two inches before it smashes through the doors of a heart
and takes another one down

this job is all we have to protect us

there is only this job between us
and the man stood on the corner of Edgware Rd and Praed Street
outside the Metropole Hotel
holding his hands out to passersby
who are heading towards their jobs

there is only this job between us
and the lady sat on the corner of Edgware and Marylebone Rd
crouched between the phone box and M&S
unable to hold out her polystyrene cup anymore
because she's gotten so tired from the night spent exposed to the cold
that she's fallen asleep
with her chin on her chest

there is only this job between us
and the man who goes along Edgware Rd every morning at 6 am
scurrying through the bins to see if he can find any food to eat
or any cigarette butts with half an inch left on them
to smoke

there is only this job between us
and the man who has all of his life tied up in blankets
knotted together with string,
who walks up Edgware Rd to the soup kitchen
on the corner of Seymour Street and Marylebone Rd

there is only this job between us
and the man who knows that is just a matter of time now
before the eviction notice comes through the door
before the bailiffs come banging
starting that slide into becoming one of those men and women
dotted along Edgware Rd

there is only this job
that we can't stop moaning about
that keep our women in love with us
and our children sat on our laps
these jobs
that keep us inches away from insanity
which give us beds and wine to soften us up every night
just so we can go out and do it all over again
tomorrow

and they wonder
why when they threaten to take them away
we get so agitated
and angry

dealing with the anger

the men who own hands
that'll never pull a pair of silk socks over their feet
the men who own throats
that'll never feel the contents of a £100 bottle of wine
slip down them
the men who own mouths
full of teeth that keep them awake at night
knowing that they'll never be able to afford
to get them filled
or capped
the men who own habits
who come in every morning
twitching like something caught in a trap
only to turn into swollen superstars
after their mid-morning snort
the men who own council tenancies
with years of service stored inside their hearts
who live in constant fear
of the new automated allocating system
taking away their jobs and their homes
the men who own memories
of what it was like to be young and fearless
with only iron in your heart and fire in your guts
who now
whenever a supervisor comes out
to bollock them for fucking up a job
lower their heads
and dig their nails into the palms of their hands
because that was the best way they knew
the only way they knew
how to stop the guts that they still had left
from making them do something
that might place all of what they believed in and loved
at risk

our fingertips

our fingertips move like lightning across their keypads
our fingertips are the tools
of our trade they move back and forth
information that our toes and ears don't feel
our fingertips are attached to our hands
they are the fingertips they crush with chains
with pincers and hours
they are under interrogation our fingertips
are on the run they are
scratching at the earth
trying to make the tunnel big enough
so that everything else behind them can follow
our fingertips are the pickaxes of their Gulags
their owners sit in rows
tapping away at their keypads
these owners who haven't owned these fingertips
for years
for centuries
made to feel guilty that their fingertips are alive
made to feel ugly that their fingertips are unique
when they should all just be mucking in
part of their collective
with this company's heart as their heart
with this company's blood in their blood
our fingertips who have no other way to exist
other than this way of theirs
who never get to share in its profits
but who always seem to get to share
in its losses

dragging our knuckles across the bone-littered floor

if we can plant our feet on the surface of the moon
and see into the back rooms of the Universe
only using a piece of glass
if we can put our eyes inside the tip of a cable
so that they can be taken down
into the depths of the ocean
if we can slip
slivers of metal into the side of a phone
that turns them into circuses
into market squares
then why can't we muster the will
to create systems in which everybody
has a job that pays them enough money
to put water and food
into the mouths of their families?

if we can split something invisible to the naked eye
and release what's left
so that it can power whole cities with electricity and heat
light and communication
then why can't we erect roofs
to go over every head in those same
cities too?

if we can spend thousands of pounds
to travel halfway around the globe
just to save a single chimpanzee
if we can all pull together
to save minke whales
stranded on a beach
if we can bring back to life
almost dead species
using just the fierce love
that we carry around inside us

then why can't we show
the same humility and grace
to the woman sat on the corner of Edgware Road
who has spent so many hours exposed to the cold
that she has completely shut down
and fallen asleep
with her chin on her chest
and her hands held out?

if we can excavate a piece of rock from the Antarctic
and peer into it
using lasers and spectrometers
only to be able to predict the exact age of the Universe
to within one single century
if we can
predict
where all of the stars and planets in this Universe will be
at any stage over the next 4 billion years
to within 0.01% of accuracy
then why were we unable to predict
that when it came to each other
we would remain cavemen
dragging our knuckles across the bone-littered floor?

one block of council flats left

just one block of council flats remains in this area
where we work our magic in
allocating out jobs to couriers
so that multinationals and £500 an hour law firms
and hedge fund managers who look after billions of pounds
can remain healthy and strong
making more money in one hour
than all the tenants of this last block of council flats left
will make in their lifetimes
put together

just one ugly block of brick and red cladding council flats still stands
amongst all of the million-pound lofts
and chrome and smoked-glass luxury flats
that have sprung up in this area over the last 8 years just one
block with 42 flats
where couriers and mechanics and schoolteachers and bus drivers
and nurses and firemen and waitresses can still safely keep
a roof over their families' heads where they can
still wash and cook and put their children into a bed
and get them up to go into a school this one block of flats left
sat there like a rotten tooth in a row of perfect molars
housing these workers
enabling them to keep their dignity and love as millionaire footballers
move in next door as seven-figure-waged bankers buy whole floors
just so they can have somewhere to stay while in London
as people in the media hire cranes
to lift £30,000 pieces of furniture into their lofts as
politicians and councillors plot
how best they can make this last ugly block of council flats
disappear
along with its infections

we march in silence

we sign the petition that comes around, that is going off to the Prime Minister raging against the years of neglect that led to Grenfell

we sign the petition online, raging against the closure of Ladbroke Grove library so that a private prep-school can take its place

we read that the councillor who made that decision already had his 3-year-old child enrolled in that school

but we march in silence

we take walks in our lunch hours around the area and see the skyline littered with cranes, that at night look like the red eyes of a sky monster

the same cranes that are rebuilding this area, after it has been pulled down and evacuated, with chrome and glass balconies that have million-pound price tags attached to each flat

but we march in silence

we live in flats all of our lives; flats that our mothers and grandmothers lived in on tenancies that they owned but which now will be passed onto our children for a period of 5 years before they get reviewed out of them and moved onto the streets

but we march in silence

we see our old youth clubs being knocked down, our libraries shut, our playgrounds shut, the same playgrounds we played kiss-chase in and smoked our first cigarette in, drunk our first can of beer in, playgrounds our children cannot play in anymore because there are construction workers in them turning them all into more blocks of luxury flats

but we march in silence
not because we aren't angry
not because we aren't raging
but because we hope that everyone else will understand
that it is because we have no voice anymore

where cranes now stand

where we once played round robin 5-a-side football competitions
that were our world cups
pulling on Argentina or Holland tops
and shorts that just about kept in our balls
where we once spent countless hours trying to impress groups of girls
with our clothes haircuts trainers smiles
the position in our pack of boys
working our way up
so that we actually got to kiss our first girlfriends
in an alcove while pretending to play a game of chess
where we drunk our first can of beer
smoked our first cigarette
tied our first ribbon after running our hands through a girls' hair
where we once picked up books
and spoke about the great things we were going to achieve
cranes now stand
cranes who've had their feet bolted into our earth
who will lift everything needed
to make another block of luxury flats
that spread out far and wide
or at least until the horizon
cranes now stand
gleaming under the sun
their lights threading the night sky
like the red eyes of a sky monster
readying this block of flats on our land
for people to come
people who haven't ever lifted a finger
to make one single thing
with their hands
who board jets to fly halfway around the globe
to sit on beaches sipping at drinks
whenever life gets too much for them
this land
where our old youth club used to stand

where knowledge was accumulated instead of bought
where we felt our first kisses turn our insides into molten heat
butterflying our guts
where we learnt how to grow up
placed our feet on that road towards becoming men and women
cranes now stand
building a complex that will hang signs around its perimeter walls

'Private Property – No Loitering!'

'NO BALL GAMES – £50 FINE!'

where the young
will not be welcome
have to stand around on street corners outside kebab shops in stairwells
steal
night hours here and there in flats where parents have had to go off to
work
the young
who soon won't have any youth clubs left anymore
to play football in
to learn how to tie ribbons in a girl's hair in
use the cover of a game of chess to learn how to kiss in
place their feet on that road
where cranes now stand
blocking their way forwards

similarities

in between taking down jobs over the phone
some of the younger telephonists talk to each other about boys
and their gym classes and their calorie intake and their plans for holidays
in Ibiza
or about nights out on the up coming weekend
wanting to know if their colleagues
experience the same frustrations and joys
sympathising and laughing when they identify in each other
shared emotions bonding and swapping numbers
Snapchat and Instagram tags
until all of them feel warm and comforted
knowing that they are all connected
thinking that they will most probably keep these friendships for years
even when they leave this company
they will stay in contact
and some of them will actually end up travelling around the world
together
or flat sharing where they will compete with each other
in drinking contests and love and heartbreaks
until they become experienced and tired enough to consider themselves
women
and move in with men into flats they can barely afford
and have children they can barely afford
until the trying to make it happen day in and day out
all of the god damn fucking time
gets inside them and begins wearing them down
and then they will start to drink a bit more
and worry a bit more
and eventually they will break up with their men
and go back to live with their mums
in flats they were brought up in
to have breakdowns
trying to work out where and why
it all went wrong

in fact
very much like all of the controllers
sat in the room opposite
who consider themselves to be men

the telephonist who works over 36-hours a week

there is a hole in her hull and she is tilting in the harbour
unable to go out to sea anymore
she is letting in water
and every month the hole just gets bigger
she has a leaking hull
and she doesn't know what to do
the system doesn't seem to want to allow her
to fix it
because after she has paid the mooring costs
and the interest on the loan she took out
to buy a new set of sails
there is never enough left over to buy
any wood and nails, tar and brushes
that can help her patch it up, stem the flow
of the water

all she wants
is to become seaworthy again
but it seems the system is designed
to make the hole even bigger
so that more water can get in
ruining her furnishings
and spoiling all of the food on board
so that there is nothing left to sleep on
or eat anymore
now that she is in this mess
the system doesn't seem to want to allow her
to mend her hull
preferring instead
to let her tilt even more
until she finally takes on so much water
that she will go under
and sink to the bottom of the harbour
along with the rest of the wrecks

the football match

at the football match the controllers arranged
against the Brazilian couriers
Marcus laid on a couple of his dads' wallpapering tables
to display the scores of litre bottles of cider
and the bucket-full of oranges
which he had bought from Sainsbury's
an hour before
and as they all began arriving for the 11 am kick-off
everyone gathered around those cider tables
swapping pleasantries and threats
about what they were going to do to each other on the field of play
before the Brazilians retreated behind their goal
to discuss positions and tactics leaving the controllers
to amble around the cider tables aimlessly smoking cigarettes
cussing the Brazilians and laughing
at their fellow teammates disarray
as behind that goal
every last one of the Brazilian couriers
stripped down into the crispest yellow blue and white Brazilian kit
and started doing keepey-upeys and amazing tricks with the ball
that took our breath away
while the controllers got changed into an assortment
of grubby club colours and favourite band t-shirts
every last one of them puling on a pair of baggy-kneed tracksuit bottoms
to shield their legs
from the cold

10 minutes after the kick-off
after it had become clear that the Brazilian couriers
were going to win by at least 20 goals
Stevie turned up
the only controller who had any pedigree
having played semi-professional for the couple of years before he
joined Phoenix Express
stripping down into his beloved Millwall kit

before jumping up and down on the spot
tucking his knees right up into the centre of his chest
running up and down ferociously in anticipation
only to then have to suddenly stop
and bend over
clutching his stomach
before puking litres of last night's alcohol and kebabs
all over the place

some people just take these things
a little bit more seriously than others
I guess

Brazilian men

the Brazilian couriers made mincemeat out of the controllers
in the football match
held over on the astroturf pitch under the Westway
they literally toyed with them
leaving the controllers heaving and gasping for air
as they played clever one-twos and sprayed the ball around
continually hitting sixpence targets with 30 and 40-yard passes
as the controllers floundered and stood there freezing
under the January sun
admiring the skill and movement of these men born in favelas
who once had no choice but to run drugs or guns for gangsters
these men
who once kicked a ball about in the slums of Rio and Sao Paulo
wanting to be the next Socrates or Zico these men
who ended up in this country delivering documents
for big banks and big lawyers and big government
who now find themselves on this astroturf pitch under the Westway
playing against men who during the week order them around
allocating out work to them
totally in control of how much will be on their pay-cheque
at the end of the week
but who for the first time
are maybe starting to realise
that there might be a lot more to these Brazilian men
other than just being couriers

after the match

after the match
the Brazilian couriers shook the hands of all the controllers
with big beaming smiles on their faces
knowing that they had inflicted a heavy defeat on these men
who during the working week held their livelihoods in their hands
and they gathered with the heaving and exhausted controllers
around the cider table
drinking from the same litre bottles of cider as them
laughing and joking at just how unfit the controllers actually were
some of them inviting the controllers back to their uncle's restaurant
where they promised roasted meats and rice and beans
with fried eggs on top
and more beer and cachaça
than even a controller could drink

this football lark
had done more in 90 minutes
than any number of those controller/rider meetings
that the supervisors insisted we all attended
outside of our paid shifts
had ever done

Sweet Claudio and the mother-fucking-son-of-a-bitch supervisor

Sweet Claudio is at the hatch going crazy
because he hasn't been paid his £500 5-day-guarantee
on account of him only working 4-days last week
but that is not stopping Claudio calling the supervisor trying to
explain this to him
a mother-fucking-son-of-a-bitch
or threatening his controller with his life
for not sorting it out
like he said he would

Sweet Claudio is in the throes of being transported back to his favela
where he had to fight and hustle for every last real
where any dip in your respect levels
resulted in hordes of other attempts
to peel you
and take from you
or even kill you

Sweet Claudio
who once asked me to lay on a Luton van
so he could move that extra-large freezer that had become available
into his home
so he could store the 60 loaves of bread
the 40 bags of chips
the 20 boxes of burgers
the 15 boxes of fish fingers
that his family of 7 kids
and beautiful wife
went through each month

Sweet Claudio
is in a rage
because he won't have enough money now
to keep that freezer full

or keep the electricity key topped up
or buy shoes for one of those 7 kids
or pay for his wife's tango lessons,
'which is the only thing she looks forward to each week',
because he thought
that his positive attitude
and infectious personality
had convinced his controller
to get that 5-day £500 guarantee paid
even though he had worked only 4

Sweet Claudio
hadn't bargained
on that mother-fucking-son-of-a-bitch supervisor
overruling the controller at the very last minute
and who is unfortunately paid
not to give a fuck about Sweet Claudio
or his 7 kids
or his beautiful wife

mother-fucking-son-of-a-bitch supervisors
are notoriously known
not to believe in love
or understand
what supplying tango lessons to a beautiful woman
can mean to a man

language difficulties

on Friday mornings
the Brazilian couriers come to the hatch to collect their cheques
and whenever the figure written down on their cheque
is what they expected
they bump my fist after I have handed it over to them
before smiling their big teethed mouths at me as we hold eyes together
and communicate about family and weather and football
laughing with each other sometimes even feeling like
we are all in this together.

on Friday mornings
the Brazilian couriers come to the hatch to collect their cheques
and whenever the figure written down on their cheque
is not what they expected
they keep their teeth in behind their lips and look at me
like I have wronged them
like they can't seem to understand
why I have done this to them
and when I try to communicate with them,
explain to them,
that they haven't got what they thought
because they didn't do their 5-day 50-hour week
to qualify for their £500 guarantee
they look at me
as though I am speaking an unknown language
cocking their head left and right at me
like an Alsatian
trying to work out why I am doing this to them
walking away after I have finished explaining
with such a sad and defeated look on their face
that even I
feel like I have somehow fucked them over
too.

the week before he died

the Friday before
he was up the hatch querying why his pay was £100 short
his controller explaining to him
that it was because he only did 4 days the week before
rather than the 5 which would've qualified him
for his £500 guarantee

getting angry and chucking his weight about wasn't his style
instead he spoke calmly almost gently with his controller
asking him if he thought that was fair
given that he had worked the previous 5 months without missing a day
he didn't think it was fair
to have £100 stopped for having a day off
because he had to take his son to the hospital
trying to reason with his controller asking him
if he thought that was fair asking him to remember
the times when he was stuck on a job going miles away
which he did without any 'moanings'
asking his controller to remember the bad weather days
when half of the fleet disappeared
but he remained driving his bike through the wind and rain
helping out
always helping out
doing whatever his controller asked

his controller
who had already tried to have him paid for that day
telling him that it wasn't his decision
but that it had been decided
that he wasn't going to get that £100

he now
taken with emotion
almost in tears
pleading with his controller
telling his controller how much that £100 meant to him
how much he needed that money
because he had an upcoming trip back to Brazil with his family
their first in over 4 years
but still had the rent and the bills to pay

a family who now a week later
are mourning the loss of its provider
the loss of its father
after sat on his bike at a pair of traffic lights
he was driven into by a Transit van
doing 30 miles an hour

a family who still have that rent
and those bills to pay
who were now going to have to cancel
that trip back to their homeland
and learn to live
without the man who missed
just one day in 21 weeks
and never got paid for it

the most beautiful vultures in the world

every Friday
when the couriers get paid
they are in the yard –
3 or 4 insurance women
dressed in tight-fitting business suits;
short skirts, jackets with deep Vs,
blouses one extra button undone,
flirting with the bike riders flush with pay
with their faces perfectly made up
and their policies bull-clipped to their clipboards
smiling all the time
like something who holds a placard up in front of a grand prix car
or something who holds up a number
and walks around a boxing ring in between rounds
looking at the riders staring back at them
giving them that smile
as though they know what they are thinking
but don't mind anyway
laughing off the chat up lines
with one-liners to disarm the profane
making comments about what they've heard
about men with big bikes
resting with such perfect precision up against those big bikes
that their skirt-hems only ever rise
enough to reveal 3 millimeters of their stocking tops
all the time knowing
that the only reason they are there in the first place
is because 1 out of the 50 couriers in front of them
will be dead or maimed by the end of the year
and that those odds
placed against the inflated premiums they charge
represent better odds of making a living
than anything else their heart's and self-respect
will allow them to do

the thousands of men

the thousands of men who have sat upon motorbikes
or inside the cabins of vans
leased them by Phoenix Express
covering hundreds of thousands of miles
paid at 70 pence each.

the thousands of men who have tried to make a living
from steering the wheels of their vans and bikes
through the streets of London,
along the motorways and lanes
of this Kingdom,
so that the packages of the great and important companies
arrive on time.

the thousands of men who have missed their child's birthday,
who have missed school plays and dinners with their families
because they have had to accept jobs going over 200 miles
at the back-end of their shifts
just so they can get those extra paid miles
onto their pay cheques.

the thousands of men who have listened
to their controllers' instructions
and put their foot down
driving through the golden glow of empty motorways
at half-past midnight
turning off into nowhere,
into the darkness of the rulers' lanes,
knowing that they will have to return
and log on for work by 9 am the next morning
if they want to keep hold of their attendance related bonus.

the thousands of men who have spilt the blood and sweat
that their parents gave them
who now have to buy £10 wraps of speed just to keep them awake,
just so they can keep going on and on
accumulating enough paid miles
that eventually will equate into a pay-cheque
that they can put into a pair of her hands
which will hopefully stop her from laughing at them
or thinking
that they are no more than slaves.

a dead deer in the back of his van

when Victor Six-Six-Five was pulled over by the police
at 3 am on a Sunday morning
and found to have a dead deer in the back of his van
which he claimed had ran out in front of him
as he was driving through Richmond Park
questions were asked and eventually he was arrested
for the attempted theft of the Queen's property
and while he was awaiting his court appearance
every time he had to come up to the office
to collect something from the control room
the controllers would start beating their fists on their desks
and rattling anything tin or metal they could get their hands on
against the steel arms of their chairs
all the while singing out 'freeee-ee Victor Six-Six-Fiiiiivve'
to the tune of the Free Nelson Mandela song
before somebody finally getting up
and going over to see what he was actually there for
commenting as they approached
that as far as they were concerned
he was a fucking hero
a rebel and a revolutionary to rival Trotsky
asking him loud enough for the whole control room to hear
if he had in the back of his van
any good quality bear-heads for sale

though the controllers and couriers
seemed to be engaged in this constant battle most of the time
don't think that when one of their couriers
got in trouble with the police
that their controllers wouldn't show them
any respect or support

Johnny No-Legs

Johnny No-Legs was dangerously red
and his eyes were always dull
and he was short
and he had a long beard
and his face always looked as though it was startled and amazed
that you were talking to it

you could feel it trying to digest
what you were saying to it
only to give up halfway through your sentence
and just grin back at you
hoping that you would understand

we got complaint after complaint from the customers
about there being a courier of ours in their reception
stinking of drink
resembling a tramp
but no one ever did anything about it
much like no one ever does anything about
global warming
or a dripping shower head

Johnny No-Legs was just there
at the back of everybody's mind
like a problem nobody wanted to confront
hanging on
as best he could
just like the rest of us

the bed and breakfast place

the bed and breakfast place
that took up all of the floors above the three shops and pub
three streets down from the office
has shut down

the bed and breakfast place where some of the couriers
down on their luck or in between homes
used to take out one-week rents
so that they had somewhere to come back to after their 11-hour shifts
to dry their leathers and undershirts on the Victorian radiators
that creaked and hissed all night
where they were able to drink themselves warm again
or heat up soup on gas rings before
laying down in a bed with one hand still gripped to the ladder
has shut down
because the landlord has decided
that it'd be better to sell the 33 years left on the lease
to property developers

it will not be long
before the three shop owners and owner of the pub decide to do the same
and the developers can then knock it all down
realising the plans they've already submitted to the council
to build another glass and marble block of luxury flats
and then they will hang million-pound price tags
from the silver and smoked-glass balconies
and then the couriers and mechanics
and other men and women
who relied on that bed and breakfast place
while down on their luck or in between homes
will have had their grip on the ladder prised open
a little bit more,
some of them completely,
but nobody will see them falling,
nobody will see them disappearing below the surface

or worry what they will do
to stop themselves from drowning

all that will happen
is people will comment on how the area
is changing for the better
and turn their eyes away
as they disappear
under the water

million-pound smiles

Whiskey Six-Two, 6 foot 4 and as muscular as a Greek god
finishes work at 4 pm every Friday
because he has a Friday night and weekend job
and we let him get away with this
because during the rest of the week
he does everything we controllers ask of him
without any moans or bitching
with an upbeat voice and a million-pound smile

his stage name is 'Marvellous Marvin'
as apparently he likes to sing along to Gaye's songs
as he peels off the layers
before beginning to swing his cock about
and smothering it in UHT cream

Whiskey Six-Two, 6 foot 4 and as muscular as a Greek god
is at the hatch
with his strange opal-blue eyes and million-pound smile
telling us that he can't work today
because he received a call the night before from a lady in Lowestoft
who he'd performed for last week
advising him that it would be better that he went to the clinic
to get himself checked out
rather than work today

as his controllers
it was our duty to tell him that missing a days' work would cost him
his £50 attendance bonus
but that was okay for Whisky Six-Two

everything was okay for Whisky Six-Two

even getting a job at 6 pm into the depths of Kent
or the furthest point of Essex
was okay for Whisky Six-Two

some people are like this
their million-pound smiles seem to make them able to resist things
that the rest of us
can't
and no one knows where it comes from
or how it exists
which I guess is a good thing
because if they did
then they'd hunt that down too

Tomas, Lima One-One-Eight

after 18 months of almost perfect service
working up to 15-hours a day
because he was needed and trusted
and had become the 'go-to-man' for us controllers
whenever we had an out-of-hours job to cover
that required his big extra-long-wheel-base
high-top van and
3 months after being asked for a divorce
by his 7-year-long wife
because he wasn't spending anywhere near enough time at home
to be considered a husband
never mind a father
to the two kids she had been left to bring up
Tomas, Lima One-One-Eight
was sacked
after it was found out
that he was living out of the back of his van.

the workshop manager
had to stand by and watch
as Tomas emptied the van of all of his belongings
onto the roadside
outside of the workshop.

1 pillow
1 foam mattress
1 sleeping bag
1 Davy lamp
1 heating element
2 red coffee cups – both chipped
1 pint of full-fat milk – 1 curdled and gone off
a black bin-liner stuffed full of clothes
a small Nescafe jar
a medium sized teddy bear with one arm missing
the leftovers and wrappings of a Chicken Cottage dinner

6 empty beer cans – all partly crushed
1 empty and 1 quarter-full litre bottle of White Lightning
a picture of two kids with their arms around each other
an empty rucksack
4 lighters
and a kerosene lamp

it seems
that some of the people
hadn't quite got their lives in order
or fulfilled 'this fabulous opportunity'
that had been presented to them
when they first picked up a set of keys
to drive one of Phoenix Express' vans.

just dip your shoulder and charge

all of the self-employed couriers
who didn't know exactly what they would get paid
at the end of the week
who only had an approximation in their minds
of the total amount they would be able
to put into a pair of her hands

all of the self-employed couriers
who are at the mercy of traffic wardens
and CCTV cameras,
who have no hearts
no souls,
who administer 60 and £130 fines
which will take those same self-employed couriers
at least 10 to 12-hours of graft
just to earn back

all of the self-employed couriers
who have to wait for jobs to be sent them
by controllers who have their own ideas
on the allocation process
while they sit in their comfortable controllers' chairs
knowing exactly what will be on their pay-cheques
at the end of the week

all of the self-employed couriers
with so much stacked against them,
with so much relying on everything
but themselves,
who get into their vans
or jump
onto the seats of their motorbikes each morning
feeling like they still have a chance
to make it

Victor Eight-Nine

Mohammed, Victor Eight-Nine, let his controller know
that his rent remained unpaid and that he didn't have the money
for his electricity bill or to eat
never mind feed his family
and that he was thinking of 'driving his van into the river' because
he was working upwards of 14-hours a day
and didn't seem to be going forward in any way.

his controller brought Mohammed's words
to his supervisor's attention
who told him to bring him up to the office
so he could speak to him
'before he does anything stupid'.

the controller got Mohammed up to the office
and showed him into the supervisor's office
and it was only 5 minutes later before the supervisor
had Mohammed by the scruff of his neck
and was walking him through the control room
with the keys to his van in his hand.

20 minutes later the police arrived at the hatch
asking why there was a man in the street
threatening to kill himself.

the supervisor explained what had happened
and the police went away
but Mohammed stayed on for hours afterwards
standing on the street outside the office
trying to convince everyone who passed
that he was going to 'do it'
because even though he'd put all of those hours in
nobody seemed to give a shit about him
or how he was struggling

and that now
even though he was threating to commit the most monstrous thing
they still didn't even seem to care
or give a damn.

he was right about one thing
nobody really did give a damn about Mohammed
they were far too busy
trying to find ways in which they could suffocate the guts
he was currently displaying.

when Mohammed came back

after the police called us up one Friday afternoon
telling us that they had pulled over one of our couriers
in Shaftesbury Avenue
and that he was telling them that he was thinking about
'killing himself'
because of the pressure his controller
was putting him under

after Mohammed
had told his controller
that he was thinking of 'driving his van into the river'
and after he had sent text messages telling his controller
that 'he knew what his game was'
that 'he knew what he was up to'
that 'he might want destroy him
but in doing so
you will also be destroying my family
so I hope you like that
Mr Controller,
I hope you like that
power'
all of which
the controller showed to his supervisor

after Mohammed
was pulled up to the office
and dismissed by the supervisor
for obviously being 'mental'
and was not to be trusted anymore
to sit behind the wheel of one of Phoenix Express' vans
Mohammed came back
2 days later
and stood at the hatch
waving a note from his doctor in the air
screaming at us all that he had proof

that he wasn't mad after all
and that he wanted the keys to his van back
so he could keep on working
and feeding his family
which was what he only ever wanted to do
in the first place

a set of dead mans' keys in his hand

when we received news
that Mohammed had somehow gained access
to the roof of Trellick Tower
and had actually jumped off

when we received news
that Mohammed had actually done
what he had threatened us all he would
and what the supervisor
had dismissed him for
before he did it in one of our company vans

when we received news
that Mohammed had checked out
because he was unable to do it anymore
none of us even considered
the man who was now going to have to carry
a set of dead mans' keys in his hand
none of us even thought
about this man who would now have to sit
in the same seat that Mohammed sat in
trying to get enough paid miles onto his pay-cheque
so that he could pay his rent and feed his family
just like Mohammed wanted

none of us thought
about this man
with the same set of keys in his hand
as Mohammed held
returning home after his 11-hour shift
to throw them into a bowl on a table beside the front door
where they would lay all night
stinking of Mohammed's death

only to be picked up again the next morning
by this new driver
this new courier
who was going to go out there
with a set of dead mans' keys in his hand
just to see if he could do it any better
than Mohammed could

those who are armed with votes

in the telephonist room
during a conversation with her colleagues
about who was behind the 9/11 attacks in New York
Hannah told everyone that she had read somewhere
that it was Guy Fawkes who'd done it

while taking down international deliveries from clients over the phone
Lauren once asked her supervisor 'what is the capital of Amsterdam?'
while Claire once enquired
'how comes it costs £30 to get something delivered to Luxembourg
but only £15 to get something delivered to Paris
when Luxembourg is the capital of Paris?'

while discussing with everyone what might be at the bottom of the sea
Daniel was completely shocked and amazed
that it wasn't in fact concreted over
'so that none of the water could fall out'
like he'd thought

and Cheyenne didn't believe it
when she was told the moon wasn't actually made out of snow and ice
telling everyone that they were mistaken
because she had seen it was so
'on one of them documentaries on the Discovery channel'

they were going to have to simplify the arguments
surrounding the upcoming referendum
on whether we should leave the EU or not
maybe even reducing them down to just one hot topic
like immigration or the NHS
or what colours should remain on our national flag
if they were going to get our telephonists to understand
what the fuck they should be voting for
in the first place

Harry's message

now that we have 'reclaimed our country back'
Harry, our head supervisor
wants to send a suitable post-Brexit message out
to all of our foreign couriers
letting them know
that they are not going to be mistreated
abused
threatened
or made victims of hate crime
any more than they were
before the vote

we can stop worrying now

all the Leave voters are walking around the control room
slapping the Remain voters on the back
telling them that we have finally
'reclaimed our country back'

the Leave voters tell us
that we can stop worrying now
because within 5 years
there will be less people in this city
which will mean that we will finally be able
to get our children a place in that school
that we had always dreamed of

they tell us that we can stop worrying now
because by the time we get old enough to need operations
or home help
there will be less people exploiting the system
so getting a hip replacement
will be like walking into a shop and buying a can of coke

they tell us that we can stop worrying so much
about losing our jobs now
because in a few years
there will be less people crawling all over each other
trying to get to those £7.80 an hour jobs
which will mean that the rate will be driven up
and more of them will become available

well I hope they're right on that one
because after a few more years
there might not be so many Brazilian couriers
prepared or even allowed anymore
to whizz around the streets
on less than 70p per mile
that keep these controllers
so happy at the recent news
in their current one

these supervisors these hypocrites

these men in white shirts sat in those offices
moving around numbers and altering percentages
so that they can protect their employment
these men who fill up company cars with company petrol
not having to lay out one single penny of their salary on road tax
parking fines, servicing
or replacement tyres
these menwho get 30 days paid holiday a year
a free Oyster card
and a client entertainment budget that they can abuse
taking their families out for dinner twice a week
these men who make sure that couriers never get paid too much
who keep any eye out
for any staff member they can jettison
into space
these men who continually try to file down the numbers
chopping away at 4's and 9's
so that they can fit them all inside the directors' ears
and hit those targets
receive those bonuses
these men
so sick of this culture
of people fabricating their status
so that they receive
something for nothing
so sick of the widening gap
between the privileged
and them
so sick of picking up the paper
to read about the latest
broken-in-two company
and its pension deficit
as the culprit purrs around a Mediterranean harbor
on a 10 million pound yacht
these men

who finally had the chance
to do something about it
who picked up their pencils
straightened their ties
and strode out onto the streets
only to put an X in the box
beside the name Hypocrisy
on the European referendum
ballot paper

the ground in dirt

the cleaner goes around at 9 pm every evening
tidying up the shit that the controllers couldn't be bothered
to put in the bins.
from the back wall under the 20-foot-long controller's desk
the cleaner pulls out polystyrene cups, discarded sweets, used tissues,
crumpled up crisp packets, pen lids, Gunster sausage roll wrappers
and bits of cucumber and tomato that have fallen
from the sandwiches the controllers eat
and then foot-soled into the carpet.

the cleaner washes up all the dishes and plates and knives and forks
piled up in the sink that the controllers couldn't be bothered to wash,
he cleans out the toilets and mops up the piss that the controllers
couldn't get into the urinals,
he wipes their controllers' chairs clean
and uses a scented fragrance to neutralise
the stench of their sweat,
he polishes the laminated glass-topped control desks
that the controllers have spilt coffee and sticky drinks on
until they are so perfectly slidey-smooth-clean
that you could glide a sheet of paper from one end to the other
only for the controllers to come in the next day
to moan about how the cleaner is a 'lazy-arsed son of a bitch'
who should 'fuck-off back to Colombia'
because he has forgotten to refill both of the soap dispensers
in the controllers' toilets
once again.

after 4 years cleaning up after these controllers
I guess the cleaner has just come to the conclusion
that it doesn't matter how much soap is put on offer
because there is some dirt
that is so ground in
you will never get it clean.

jokes in this workplace

the Moroccan controllers take the jokes about their uncles being
responsible for the bomb scare
that has just shut down the Chiswick flyover

the black controllers take the jokes about not offering us
a share of their crisps
because 'is it that we are black?'

the Kiwi controllers take the jokes about them obviously being gay
because they spend all of their time in boozers drinking beer
before taking off their t-shirts
and wrestling with each other

and the East European controllers take the jokes
about them all being over here
because they are obviously not as tough as the historians say they are
preferring instead
to come over here
to take our jobs and our women

in fact
the only ones who don't seem to be able to take the jokes
are the English white males
who get so prickly
when you call their mother's virtue into doubt
who get so sulky
when you call their sister's bloodline into doubt
who get so aggressive
when it is suggested that they may have a problem
with their fellow controllers
simply because they can't see more than four feet in front of them
because their eyes are obviously fucked
due to the mutation that set in
when their inbreeding took place
jokes

in this workplace
had better be racially biased
otherwise you'll never get anyone to understand them
never mind
laugh at them

how many shifts must a controller put in before he picks up a saxophone or pen

how many shifts must a controller put in before he realises
that this country he calls his own has disowned him
and couldn't care less if he starved
or even if he didn't have a roof to cover his head
how many hours does a controller have to put up with
getting screamed and shouted at by supervisors paid 4 times more
just because he wasn't able to get the forgotten passport of a CEO
delivered back into his hands
before his flight took off so he could board that flight
and fly halfway around the globe to sign a contract that will level a forest
flood a plain cause
whole communities to have to move on
before
that controller realises
that the migrants he blames for taking all of the flats
for draining the treasury of his tax pounds in undeserved benefits
are not the problem
but that the government he voted in who he sings songs for
whose national flag he has had tattooed on his calf
are

how many hours of toil and pressure must the controller endure
before he accepts
the reason why his pay cheque still says the same as it did in 2012
is not because of the migrant workers flooding their streets living under
every manhole cover eating
everything green hanging from the trees raping
and grooming their daughters that
the real reason why
are the policies of this country he beats his chest for buys team-shirts of
stands
in pubs rowing with mates about who had the greatest empire
ever on earth

how many youth clubs libraries and post offices
need to be knocked down to be replaced by blocks of luxury flats
before that controller stops blaming those same immigrants
for taking all of the flats and all of the NHS beds for him to realise
that he's been part of a magic trick a hypnosis that has just
convinced him
they are
how many cranes
need to stand guard in the sky
waiting to lift block of marble after block of marble glistening handrail
after glistening handrail
air-conditioning ventilation water sprinkler jacuzzi steam room
and shower systems
up to the top floors of those luxury flats before that controller
lays down his anger and stops blaming the Somalian Brazilian
Colombian Nigerian East European black
man and black woman Muslim and Jew
and picks up a saxophone or a pen
to announce to the world that he has finally understood
and wants to link arms with all of his sisters and brothers
whatever their skin

putting on those 40 grand a year chains

for 40 grand a year
you can't let it be known by the supervisors
that you are bitching along with the rest
for 40 grand a year
you can't go into HR and complain
that you are being singled out for too many weekend shifts
even if you are
for 40 grand a year
you can't throw down your headset anymore
and scream into the ceiling about how dumb the couriers are
driving around the streets at ridiculous speeds
missing collection after collection
for 40 grand a year
you can't ignore the dress code of black trousers and smart shirt
that makes you stick out amongst all of the 25 grand a year
controllers
in their jeans and t-shirts
like an SS officer
for 40 grand a year
you have to fight back the urge
to rub snot around the spout of the supervisor's coffee machine
you have to listen and pretend interest
as the supervisor tells you about his weekend away in the Cotswolds
for 40 grand a year
you have to convince everyone
that the sun is made out of diamonds and ice
and that what we are doing
is looking for little chips of it
that get blown down to Earth on the solar wind
for 40 grand a year
you have to move mountains in the name of Phoenix Express
because that is your religion and your Father
because on 40 grand a year
they own you
they own your skin and everything in it

they own the feet in your socks
they own the holiday brochures your woman thumbs through
they own the new set of car keys she wants dropped into the palm of
her hand
they own your kids' affection
your self-esteem
your happiness
and your fear
which on 40 grand a year sits inside your ear
constantly muttering,
'you better not fuck this one up, Buster'

40 grand a year
is the hook they use
to drag you over the line
into that dirty dead-dark sea
where what was just a job before
has now suddenly become your new addiction
your new master
where nothing is left to save you
or drip you any hope
other than this job
that has you in its 40 grand a year chains

Dermot, you fucking piece of shit

when Dermot took up the offer
of transferring from being a controller into being a supervisor
we all got together
and bought him a congratulations card
all writing our bits in
detailing how we thought
he had thrown himself off the edge of the world
how he was
throwing himself away into a pit of mud
how he had for years
pulled at the threads of a prostitute's dress
up and away over his head
until it had all now finally fallen away
revealing everything
and him there now diving into it

we all saw him there
playing the game perfectly
until he got made into a supervisor

and now he is earning 15 grand a year more
than we are
we
who still have to keep the engine running
stoking the fires and making it tick
while he will sit around now
pouring over reports about our performance percentages
making decisions
on whether we get our bonuses or not
making decisions
on whether we have to work a weekend shift or not
learning quick
that if he is going to justify that 15 grand a year more
and be a feared and revered supervisor
then he will have to come out sometimes

and not look us in the eye
before screaming and shouting at us
that he has caught us fucking up
waving his red cape around in the air
like a superhero suddenly arriving to save the world

Dermot
you fucking piece of shit
we will be here
after you have got the money to
holiday in Thailand
after you have got the money to
buy a French bulldog
and a pair of flower cutters
we will be here
after you have had the kids
and dressed them in blue and white sailor's tunics
with little red ribbons tied on the sleeves of their arms even after
you have moved up to Highgate
and bought a yellow fridge
to match the sunshine
of your stupid dream
we
will
still be here
because nothing happens without us Dermot
nothing gets done
without these hands
that you have now
let go of

no thank you

every time a controller
goes in to ask for a rise
he is told by his supervisor
that he will have a word with the directors
and then get back to him

if the supervisor doesn't value the controller
then he will not bother getting back to him
but if he does
then the directors will call him in a few days later
over to the accounts and administration building across the road
where he will have to wait outside the boardroom
until they are ready
and when they finally call him in
they will tell him that they can give him what he wants
but only if he agrees to take on some extra responsibilities
such as making sure the weekend shifts are covered
or helping out with recruitment
or dealing with courier pay queries
before making him fully aware
that if they do give him what he wants
then sometimes
even at the drop of a hats'notice
he'd be expected to actually physically go out of the office
to visit customers

that's why controllers who have been there for more than a few years
never go in for pay rises
preferring instead to wait for their 18 month appraisals
before accepting the equivalent of 6 more bottles of wine
or 2 tickets to the cinema
or two-and-a-half weeks' more
electricity and heat

after all

having been guilty of some of the most horrendous fuck-ups
that had ruined whole events
and finely balanced deals before
the last thing any of us wanted to do
was to actually meet
one of those customers

who knows what the fuck they would do to us

the wise and the shrewd

the career controllers who had been there for years
sat there rolling their wedding rings around their fat fingers
every now and then straightening
the gold crucifixes on their gold chains
so that they hung perfectly straight
inside their thick chest hairs.

the career controllers who knew every square inch of the terrain
and how to avoid its dangers
never complained directly to the supervisors
about the piss-poor hardware
or Mickey Mouse software
or about the quality
of the couriers the company took on
all of which, it was thought
contributed to us losing our performance related bonuses
eachmonth
they liked to leave that sort of thing to everybody else
because knowing that nothing would ever get done about it
what was the point
'in fighting that battle'.

the career controllers
take lunch together
and laugh while Rome burns,
they know exactly when it is about to get busy
like it is a scent in the air that no one else can detect,
they know exactly how long they should leave alone
the new controller,
just enough so it looks like he is getting out of his depth
just enough so it looks like they have jumped in and saved it
but never enough that it might get out of control,
and if ever it does get out of control
the career controllers distance themselves
by going off to do paperwork

that they have been nagged at by their supervisors
to complete
so that when it all goes wrong
they can hold out their arms and say,
'I can't do everything, mate.'

but the real quality of the career controllers
was this ability they had
to know exactly when to walk away from a situation
seconds before its bomb explodes
and then just stand there
looking back at the mayhem
one inch out of its reach
pulling that amazed and shocked face
that has kept them in this job for years.

remaining controllers

the controllers like to question the motives behind the supervisor's entries
on the monthly rota for weekend cover,
scrutinising every placement
for any sign of unfairness
or preferential treatment

they like to question the integrity of the pay department
pulling apart the NI and tax contributions on their monthly pay slips,
mulling over how odd it is
that in all the years they've all been controllers,
'nobody ever got a tax rebate round here!'

they like to question the reduction of their lunch breaks
from 60 minutes to 40,
endlessly going on about how unfair it was
that they had no say in the matter

they like to question the decency of the supervisors
who though promising they would
never bothered to get the broken air conditioning system fixed
for 18 months
causing the controllers to freeze during the winter
and bake to gush during the summer

the controllers like to question their mechanics' abilities,
the curious delays in getting vehicles back on the road
after the controllers have called them up
telling them that they need that vehicle back on the road
urgently

they like to question the days off their fellow controllers have
when they call in sick
saying that he's not ill at all
but most probably just had a few too many the night before
sometimes even pretending that a courier is calling them up on the radio

yelling out at the top of their voice 'what's that Kilo Two-Four?
what's that...?
you've just past the Battle Cruiser on Homerton High Street
and seen Jimmy standing outside
supping on a pint!?'
before looking over at their fellow controllers
and giving them a wink

there is almost nothing beyond the questioning of a controller
they are one of the most inquisitive creatures on the planet
always out trying to dig up evidence
to prove that they are being mistreated

in fact
the only thing that controllers don't seem to question
is why
if it is all so bad and stacked against them
they remain being controllers

not yet weary enough or lucky enough, I guess

the weary and lucky controllers have mostly left
to fill niches in the building trade
or on the rubbish
or to take up jobs in facility companies
or hardware shops
with almost zero amounts of responsibility
leaving us controllers not yet sane enough to walk
with a rag-tag of young bucks
who with only 6 months to a years' experience in this control room
keep on making mistakes
causing the couriers to come up to the hatch and scream at them
causing the customers to get on the phone and scream at them
or else get on the phone to the supervisors
who will then come out and scream at them
on that customer's behalf

the young bucks
who have spent only 6 to 12 months in this control room
before being handed their headphones
and over to us
and the more we show them the less they learn
preferring instead to make their own decisions
more cocky and full of it than a silverback
sitting in those old weary and lucky controllers' chairs
flailing about over their keypads
like it is some kind of computer game
as those same lucky and weary controllers
sit in beer gardens after their 8-hour days
drinking up ale
and the sun
not understanding why
they hadn't left
even sooner

yet another leaving do

the relentless pressure placed on them by supervisors
and the relentless pressure placed on them by clients
who both seemed to want rabbit's pulled out of a hat
willy-nilly
the build up of this
with their hearts and faces pushed up against it
every single minute of their 11-hour shifts
with nowhere to go
other than to face it up
and the expectation that on top of this
they will have to do
at least one weekend shift every month
and the gradual breakdown of communication
between them and their women
and the gradual breakdown of communication
between their women and them
and the murders committed on their estates
and the murders committed inside their minds
and the way they felt that they had to get drunker each night
just to feel like they were feeling normally
and the total lack of dolphins in their bay
and the amount of favourites that came in
when they were backing long shots
and the amount of long shots that came in
when they were backing favourites
all of that
piled on top of everything else
can sometimes cause a controller to flip
and to run around the control room
kicking and punching at all of the computer screens
knocking them all onto the floor
before jumping up and down on top of them
crunching their plastic and glass
under their boots
while waving their arms about

and screaming into the stunned faces around
that they 'CAN'T TAKE IT ANY MORE!'
and the rest of us controllers
to just look at each other
and let out a sigh
realising once again
that we were going to have to attend
yet another leaving do

the men who make Phoenix Express tick

the men who make Phoenix Express tick
listen to dub and rock and thrash metal and hip-hop rap
they roll their sleeves up
and twist their arms up into their fellow controllers' faces
so that they can see that their latest tattoo
says the words NO FEAR
when viewed upside down

the men who make Phoenix Express tick
smoke weed and snort speed
they know how to assemble and administer
their drugs
they know how to keep it wide
of the supervisor's eye
always out balancing their moods
with a toke on a spliff to calm themselves down one minute
and a little line of speed
to bring them up the next

the men who make Phoenix Express tick
don't know how to be straight
always up getting themselves into mischief
always on an edge
searching for something
to balance their moods
balance their minds

the men who make Phoenix Express tick
have never seen the beauty of a cool clear morning
or stared at the sun without a fuzzy head
or leapt out of bed with gusto and vigour

no
the men who make Phoenix Express tick
are always intensely aware of their environment
and what is moving about inside it
whether it is a meal or a threat
they are always chasing something they can't quite define
or put their finger on
something that lives and breathes
away in another place
under the branches
inside the fog
somewhere
where none of them will ever find it

and all the time while they are doing this
they make Phoenix Express tick

the sun didn't rise today

Timmy was special
he used to call on for work at 7 am every morning
smack right in the centre of London
ready for anything his controller gave him
and when the jobs started coming in
he'd accept them on his PDA as quick as a flash
easing that van of his into gear, eating up the road
and by 9 o'clock
when most of the other couriers were just waking up
or else calling in for work from home
he'd already have 6 jobs under his belt
then as things started hotting up
Timmy would move into another gear
flinging that van of his around the streets
accepting everything his controller sent him
never having to use an A-to-Z or sat nav
with all of the pick-up addresses and delivery addresses
he had on his schedule
beeping away inside his head
like a holographic map
as they all moved like on a gyroscope
every time he turned that steering wheel of his
his whole mind the same as a screen
in front of a NASA control mission centre
as he suddenly turned off main roads
to scoot off down alleyways just about wide enough to take his van
snaking off through back-doubles
that not even black cab drivers knew about
only to reappear 400 yards back up on the main road
ahead of the traffic

and whenever he got to a collection or delivery address
he'd park that van of his half-on half-off of pavements
leaping out of his van in a blur
so fast he hadn't ever got a ticket in over 6 years
constantly drinking coffee from that big metal flask of his
constantly plucking sugar-coated cola-bottles from that big bag
he kept in between his thighs
flicking them up into his mouth
jabbering away on his radio
screaming at his controller, 'give me more! give me more!'
all day for 11 hours straight
without a break or anything to eat
never slowing down
relentless as a Spartan
until finally he would turn that van of his towards home
having accumulated the work of 3 men
bibbing his horn
as he headed up Tottenham Court Rd towards Camden
with over 30 jobs and £150
in his pocket

until that Monday
when he didn't call on at 7 am like he always did
everyone in the control room commenting on it
like it was the same as the sun not coming up today
all of us
finding out later that he had topped himself
sat on the balcony of his flat
where he must've decided that whatever it was
he couldn't take it anymore
and opened that vein
that usually held in all of that extra-special blood of his
blood that made him better than 3 men

Ronnie
commenting later that,
'some men
are just far more capable
of doing almost anything
than other men
I guess.'

the music that keeps these men going

the men who work in this control room
listen to various types of music
that they tell their fellow controllers
is better than the music that *they*
listen to

while they try to keep up with the amount of jobs
that keep dropping down onto their screens
their music walks through them
they whistle and hum their music
it gives them inner strength
helps them concentrate
able to keep making it happen
to keep going on

Nina Simone, Beethoven, The Jam
Bob Marley, Trojan, Amy Winehouse, Curt Cobain
their music is going on inside them all of the time
as the jobs keep dropping down onto their screens
they keep the music with them because it keeps all of the doors ajar
because it helps make them feel stronger
or something other
than what they want you to feel

the music that Marley made
the music that Whinehouse made
the music that Cobain made
that Simone made
Beethoven made
the music that Trojan and The Jam made
all going on inside the heads of the men
who work inside this control room
somehow helping them feel like they are part of something bigger
and not just robots
who punch away at keypads all day

somehow managing
to keep their minds alive
not allowing them to die
or give up
like the supervisors who walk around the control room
jabbering away about performance percentages
and service level agreements
have done

birthing season

the foals have exited from between their mother's legs
and they are fresh out of the womb.
their forelegs bent,
their knees and the tips of their noses
pinned to the dirt,
their hind legs locked-tight
up-righting their behinds into the air
trying not to let the weight of everything that is in between
pull them down
flat into that dirt.

their eyes,
shiny with fear,
look around,
hoping that nothing will come in unnoticed
and sink its teeth
into their still glistening-with-afterbirth
underbellies.

stuck-on-a-nerve trembling
they listen to the controllers mouthing their strange language
that most will never learn, never understand.
watching the controllers,
they try to copy their actions,
until finally, they think they have got it
and get up
only to fall down again
and get up
only to fall down again
and get up
only to fall down again.

this will go on for 8 months
and for those who don't get tired
of continually falling down
and having to get up again,
for those who finally begin
deciphering some of that strange language,
those
will get to run with the controllers for 11-hours a day
learn how to deal with stress-related illnesses
develop strange addictions
and get £1,800 a month
paid into their bank accounts
until all of that birthing process
will be forgotten.

apart, of course,
the constant fear
that something at any minute
might come in unnoticed,
like from the supervisor's office
or the HR department,
and sink its teeth
into their underbellies.

that fear
never leaves any of us.

no perspective

as we sit in our controllers' chairs
fretting about picking up cakes and drums of ink
fashion garments and printed documents
being pressured by our supervisors
to get them all delivered on time,
other people wonder where their next litre of water will come from
or if they will ever get the chance
to eat a piece of meat again

as we fume and steam that we have been put on the late shift
for the third consecutive week running
and take our fuming and steaming to the HR manager
demanding to know if there is some kind of plot underway
to 'manage us out of the business',
23 year old commanders
decide to machete to death whole families
just because they are from a different tribe

as we sit in our comfortable controllers' chairs
drinking coffee and tapping away at our keypads
moaning about the way our women try to dictate our lives
and how if it carries on
then we are going to have to consider
leaving that 'moany fucking bitch'
along with those two kids we fathered,
4 year olds get washed up on an Italian beach
because their families were trying to get to a land
where the woman wouldn't get raped
and the man put in a cell for over 20 years
just for stealing a kilo of flour

as we bemoan the hours we put in doing this job
placed under what we consider intolerable pressures
trying to balance the needs of the clients and couriers
having our jobs threatened each day
by supervisors we consider to be on the same rung as dictators
unable to cover the bills and debt payments each month
thinking all the time that we are not paid
anywhere near enough for what we do,
others sit in makeshift camps
or roam the streets with nowhere to go
happy at least that they are not now in their land
where their dictators chopped off the hands of a man
just for stroking the cheek of his wife
in a public square

when we come home completely stressed
from the 11-hour shifts we've put in
drinking wine, bitching
about how the supervisor only picked us up on the 4 or 5 jobs we fucked up
without taking into consideration the hundreds of others
that we made happen
falling asleep in our comfortable beds
to dream of holidays and sex,
others have trouble falling asleep at all
and dream that if only they could have the same problems
as those controllers
then they wouldn't have to cower under their beds
every time they heard a helicopter
approaching overhead

controllers
in their £400 a week take-home controlling jobs
have always had problems
getting things into perspective

getting buzzed by the CEO

the CEO
has found out that I am writing poems
about the company he owns

he has called me into his office
which is bigger than my front room
to discuss them

he is very cordial at first
hands me a glass of water
before then asking me
what got me writing
in the first place

I tell him that it felt good
getting it all down
after all of those 11-hour shifts
and that it acted like a kind of therapy
that somehow enabled me to go on and on
despite everything

he got up from his chair
prowled around his office for a bit
then sat on the edge of his desk
right in front of me

he then asked me
to define what that 'everything'
was

'you know,' I said,
'all the stresses and shit we go through each day...'
and then before I could say anything else
he asked me whether I thought
that what I have to put up with

was anything different
to what other members of his 'team'
have to put up with

'no,' I said,
but...'
and then I suddenly realised
that this office
with all its leather
and mahogany
and chrome
and cool air
was actually
a gigantic trap

and that the CEO
was a predator
and that nothing I could say
would help me
get out of it

in fact
the more I said
the more this trap
would close tighter
and tighter
around me

'I hope you don't feel
that you are special in any way
because I can tell you now
that your supervisors,
which you seem to delight so much in ridiculing,
have to put up with a whole lot more shit
than you do.'

I thought about the rent
the electricity bill
the loan repayments
the nail in the tyre of our car
and the way Christmas
made my children's eyes shine like a sun
rising up over the horizon
setting fire to the sky…

that magic bit

I'm sitting in one of those flashy coffee shops
drinking a cold brew
with whipped cream on top.
what can I say;
I'm a sinner.
and this lady starts making a fuss at the till
and it's like a flock of sparrows
lifting off from a bush
in panic.

I look at her
in her lycra,
a designer bag over her shoulder,
waving her phone about in the air,
demonstrating at the girl
behind the till.

and I wonder where
it all went wrong,
where we all lost that magic bit
that made us human
and able to tolerate
minor inconveniences.

the girl behind the till
is saying sorry
as the woman
waves her phone about in the air
getting more and more upset
until she finally
calls for the manager.

apparently
the app on her phone
that she uses to pay for her coffee
isn't working
and the woman behind the till
has told her she needs to pay cash
but the woman
has no cash on her,
'can't you see I'm on my way to the fucking gym!'"
and because she comes in every day
she wants the lady
to give her a free coffee
which she will pay for
later.

but the lady can't do that.
and that's why there is a flock of sparrows
lifting off at the till
and the manager coming.

if the apes could only see
what they have become,
what we have lost
or had stolen.

it makes me both laugh
and feel sad
which, I decide,
is the perfect mix
to go and write some poems
and drink a whole lot of wine.

like a sniper wrapped up in wine

you have to sit here patiently some nights
and not worry about Donald Trump
or the troubles in Syria
or the colour of a poppy

you have to sit here patiently some nights
and not worry about Brexit
or bullfighting
or the leaking shower head
or the way the alcoholic woman next door
keeps playing Nina Simone at full blast
into the early hours

you have to stay patient
like a tiger in the forest
moving a leaf aside with its nose
like a spider
shooting silk out of its arse
like a bluntnose shark
who feeds on a decaying sperm whale
and then won't eat again for another year

you have to sit here patiently some nights
looking at the walls
drinking wine
smoking cigarettes
with socks on your feet
and fingernails that have grown too long

nothing else is needed
just patience
and
the understanding
that you are on your own
and don't have to prove anything

you have to sit here patiently some nights
like a sniper wrapped up in wine
sometimes the words come into sight
sometimes
they don't

fuck off darlings

fuck off with your award-winning
fuck off with your writer groups
fuck off with your plastic covers of books that contain no heart
no guts
fuck off with your equations and rules
your blank little spaces that are supposed to represent a woman's
breath
a man's sweat
fuck off with your readings and open mic events
your slaps on the back
your reach-arounds
fuck off with your 'suffering' radar
it is so busy
fuck off with your dead pets your dead mothers who stitched
seahorses into your duvets and dressing gowns
and fuck off to your pieces that are so PC on-point
PC is stuck in your throats like a bunch of frogs
and whenever any of you speak
all we get is the same croak
the same storm of words
we need
a different raging
other than your obscure metaphors
your complicated words
and your irrelevant plots

we need you now
more than ever
but all you can do is paint pictures of seas crashing onto beaches
that no one will ever sit on
skies littered with stars that no one can see
silk gloves that will never be pulled onto the hands
of the men and women you punt
your dribble out at

beano

the mechanics outdid even themselves
on their latest beano down to Southend
with Scott not even making it there
detained at Loughton services
for pissing in a rubber plant next to the Cashino one armed bandits
and then Craig
falling off the pier as soon as he got there
standing up on the railings as he acted out the scene from Titanic
before a gust of wind lifted him up and over the side and Paul
passing out on a bench overlooking the sea
having drunk too much out of Smithy's flask of mushroom tea
and then after midday
Ben getting into a fight on the promenade
with the chicken mascot for Chicken Cottage
ripping his headpiece off and chucking it up into the wind
so that it careered off and landed in the lap of a child's buggy
and Brian pissing himself in between pubs
and Smithy playing the £1-a-go bingo slots
only to disappear with a woman old enough
to be his grandmother
and Liam
breaking his ankle as he tried to jump from his dodgem
into Chris's dodgem
only to fall short and get run over
by a dodgem driven by two old age pensioners

the thousands of hours spent in Phoenix Express's workshop
changing clutches and oil filters
having to lift whole engines out of vans on wrenches and pulleys using
all of their strength to lower those engines down
onto their workbench like
a feather,

the thousands of hours spent in the Siberian cold of that workshop
laying on that floor that seeped all of its cold into the bones of their backs
as they peered up into exhaust systems and suspension systems
trying to service vehicles so they could make those 130,000-mile vans
and bikes
start up like brand new machines
had obviously taken its toll on our mechanics

nothing though
that a day out at the seaside
couldn't put right

peace

the mechanics sought peace while stuck under those 130,000-mile vans
trying to clean and replace oil filters and carburettors
so that those vans could be rolled out of their workshop
as good as new
the mechanics sought peace while staring into the bikes that had been
brought into their workshop
dying
staring into their engines while their burnt and red fingers twisted back
the revs
resting their ears as close to those engines as they could possibly get
just so they could hear and feel the illnesses of those bikes
inside their guts
as their fingers twisted away and turned at the caps on those engines
trying to heal them
the mechanics
who lived in rooms within rented flats filled with men
who also sought peace
sharing their lives with men who washed cars
and moved the contents of offices into other offices
for less than the cost of a burrito
per hour
men who propped themselves up on their pillows at night seeking peace
by drinking cans of cheap beer and eating kebabs
skyping their families far away in other
countries
men who got up at 5 am every morning feeling rejuvenated
to march at the sun and swallow the universe
putting up scaffolding or delivering boxes
for men who weren't anywhere near
the men that they were

the mechanics sought peace under those 130,000-mile vans
because they didn't have a fig tree to sit under like Buddha did
the mechanics who tried to heal those dying bikes
with their fingers and hearts
because they didn't have a woman to hold at night
the mechanics who couldn't afford anything more
other than to exist in their rooms within rented flats
filled with other men all seeking the same type of peace that eagles
gliding through the immense sky feel

I don't know about you

I don't know about you
but I miss the steel strips
on the backs of chairs
outside an ice cream parlour
I miss the way
they used to eat into my back
pinch
the fat of my back together
so that when I got up
you'd have three red bars across there
like you had been branded
I liked being branded by them
in my shorts
holding my grandad's hand
that big hand
that once picked up a shovel to dig a trench in a war
nowhere near the salt and seagulls
of the sea he believed in
I liked the way his hands
made everyone turn their heads
as he dragged one of those steel chairs
across the floor
of the Queen Mary's Rose Garden
to the table I was standing at
rather than lifting it up quietly in the air
said, 'plonk you're arse on that, son'
I liked the way his big Geordie voice
made everyone stare
lift their little fingers higher
on the cups of their tea

I don't know about you
but I liked the way
the coldness of the steel
felt on my back

their uncomfortable heat in Summer
burned
the backs of my thighs
the way my grandad mocked the others
for sitting on towels
laughed out loud
when he came back with two vanilla cornets in his hands
saying, 'they only asked me
if I wanted it in tubs, son.
a fucking tub. I telled them
tubs are for bathing in man
cornets is for fucking ice cream.'

I don't know about you
but I miss that steel
and those hands
the way back then
nothing was allowed
to take anything's place
without a fight
or a demonstration

I don't know about you
but these plastic chairs we now sit on
eating our ice cream out of tubs
don't brand me
in the same way
as the salt
and the seagulls
ripped sideways across the sky
once did

no one is irreplaceable

3 months after they got rid of Horse
for breaking a courier's hand in a vice
and after the workshop spares cabinet
had very few spares left in it
because the new head mechanic
had forgotten to fax off the order
and after 3 of our best mechanics
had left in protest
and after Kilo Three-Eight's front wheel
fell off a quarter of a mile down the road
after a service
causing him to fall off his bike
and shatter his collar bone
and after it became too common an event
for couriers whose bikes had developed mechanical problems
to go into the workshop
only to never come back out again
they decided to phone up Horse
to see if he wanted his old job back

when Horse got the call
offering him his old job back
a swarm of butterflies
lifted off inside his stomach

when Horse got the call
offering him his old job back
his great big old heart
skipped a beat
and the tips of his fingers
began to throb again

when Horse got the call
offering him his old job back
he told them that he'd think about it

and would get back to them
which he did
15 minutes later

the day Horse came back
he had to come up to the control room
to go over the weekly service rota
with the supervisor involved
and as he came up the stairs
he let out this big roar
that made all of us controllers jump in our chairs
and as we looked around
he was already through the door
coming at us
with his arms held out
with his eyes poking out
coming down the length of the control room
with his mad beard swinging
letting his right arm trail-bang
into the sides of our heads
making our right ears sting

then when he got to the end of the control room
he pulled himself up
and jumped a perfect 180
landing in perfect squat
his face leaning forwards
staring at us
snorting revving-up-the-engine noises through his nose
rubbing his hands up and down his thighs
before suddenly setting off again
like a bullet roaring
attempting to slap all of the controllers' left ears
on the way back out

obviously somebody was happy
to be back

at the inquest

Horse said that he could've told us
that Kilo Two-Eight's bike
wasn't up to going to Newcastle
with such an urgent package on board,
that Yankee Five-Four's bike
had a bearing problem
that was about to go at any minute
so giving him an urgent delivery to Southampton
was stupid
and that Kilo Two-Four's bike
had two balding tyres on it
so it was obvious
that at some stage
he was going to get pulled over by the police,
it was just unfortunate
that it happened
while he had an urgent delivery on board
for the MD of a big bank.

Horse
told us all of this
as we sat around the table
going over the reasons
why we had lost 8 accounts in the last week
followed by,
'if only you had asked.'

the apprentice mechanic

when Sarah was taken on by the recruitment manager
as apprentice mechanic
without any consultation with Horse
Horse quickly got down to making Sarah
feel as uncomfortable
as possible
first he put Sarah on oil change and bike cleaning duty
which caused her overalls to become grimy and wet
and the cold material to cling against her body all day
then he insisted that because she was the 'new girl'
she would have to make coffee or tea for the rest of the mechanics
whenever they asked
which Horse got them to do regularly
then he put her on hosing down duty
and wouldn't let her go at night
until the workshop floor was completely cleaned of all the oil and grease
which it had never been before
in the whole duration of Horse's reign

the final straw though
was when Horse pulled a tampon out of the telephosts' toilet bin
and nail-gunned it to the workshop wall
under which he spray-canned the line

SARAH'S DEAD CHUFF LINING!

she left a couple of hours afterwards
but like Horse said
it was policy
the only women who ever got to stay in his workshop
we're the ones printed on glossy sheets of A4 paper
that he pulled out of magazines

Horse's asylum

Horse had 3 young kids
but he didn't moan
when we all piled around his
after the pub
after our 55-hour weeks

he'd raid his fridge
and there'd always be enough beer and wine
for everyone

his woman would come out sometimes
ask us to keep the noise down
and we'd all just stare at her
wondering how there was someone in this world
who had been able to be 6 years with Horse

when she went back to bed
Horse would just turn the music up
holding a bottle of beer to his lips
like it was a microphone
singing along to The Kinks
at the top of his voice
until she would come out again
scream at him
that he was taking the piss
that he was waking up the kids
and ruining her sleep
but he didn't care
he just picked her up in his arms
and swirled her around to the music
whispering things into her ear
that made her laugh and throw back her hair
until finally she said, 'fuck it,
give me a swig of that beer.'

and then she would sit with us
smoking cigarettes and drinking
holding Horse's hand
as later
when we were all off our heads on wine
he told us about when he was a kid
his insane father
and the asylums he used to have to go
visiting him at

our guts and our hands

he invited me back to his houseboat for drinks some weekends
and we'd sit there
on the top of it
smoking and drinking wine
and I'd listen to this man who was dying of cancer who had spent
50 years in the system of work
who had the letters S-C-A-V-E-N-G-E
tattooed across the fingers of his hands
telling me about how we should
never give up raging
never give up fighting
until the day we die
because that was exactly what they wanted us to do
telling me it was an imperative
that we keep on standing up
after getting knocked down
raging
rattling the bars of our cages
because raging was our only hope
as he turned up The Who on his portable stereo
telling me to be careful
because a man in a rage should choose his battles carefully
and never let his heart get strung out
fighting on too many fronts
because they'll end up eating him up
and make him feel like it is all his own fault
that he feels like he is going insane

then after she'd put the kids to bed
his girlfriend came up to join us
and we'd all sit together on the top of his boat
smoking and drinking wine
laughing together
realising at about 2 am
that our guts and our hands
were the only things we had left
to hold on to

stitching this Universe together

Sadiq wants to stay a part of this control room, a part
of this bunch of chained cynical indebted men
who continually take the piss out of his haircuts
his shoes and his love life
who never cut him any slack whenever he makes a mistake
laughing and calling him names that Sadiq laughs back at
because Sadiq knows
that he will be a part of that pack in a couple of hours
and that the hands he uses to twist the shoes onto his 2-year-old's feet
every morning
and that wrap the scarf around her neck to keep her warm
and that slip her coat over her shoulders by the door
are the same hands as Mikey's and Bill's and Dermot's and Javed's
who every morning slip and wrap the same shoes and scarves and coats
around their children

Antoine wants to stay a part of this control room, even when it is him
who is on the receiving end of his fellow controllers' cruelty
taking the mickey out of him getting bollocked by one of the supervisors
as they circle and sharpen their minds
waiting for the quietest moment possible
before launching their one-liners and cusses
into his ears
causing the rest of the pack to crack up in fits of laughter
because Antoine knows that all of this
is done in the name of survival
a survival that enables Antoine to put cereal on the table
in front of his 6-year-old boy pour
milk into his wife's coffee cup keep
the car topped up with diesel the lights burning the roof solid the water
hot the sun up in the sky
warming all of our hands and backs as we punch buttons on keypads lift
quarter ton engines out of vans haul
filing cabinets from one office into another office
and all because

we need to protect those castles
that we can safely pack our lives away in
whenever it gets cold

Stacey wants to stay a part of this control room
where despite all of the bollockings and bloodlettings
she has been on the end of
she keeps getting up after being knocked down
constantly talking with enthusiasm about her end games, her outs
which this control room is going to give to her
which has her sitting on beaches lying next to Calvin Klein models
balancing Campari and sodas on their ripped stomachs
or behind the steering wheel of a 35-grand sports car
heading into a sunset the colour of a burning boys' heart
or sat on the edge of a pool
dangling her feet in the water behind her paid-for home
with the sun holding her hand
and the ocean salting her hair
the same dreams in fact
that the woman sitting next to you on the bus has
that the woman typing figures into a computer terminal all day has
that the woman who scans your shopping at the checkout has
that the man sat at the top of a crane or in the cabin of a van has
the same dreams of freedom that we all have
where we won't anymore have to put up with a man
who feels the need to dehumanise and bully us
in front of a room full of people
just because he is paid 4 times more
and has a reputation to keep

we all want to stay a part of this control room
for as long as possible
or at least until our hands cannot tap one single button more
on one of their keypads
or at least until our minds have given up
and can't see through the hundreds of jobs
that keep dropping down onto our screens
or at least until our blood

stops foaming with this adrenalin
which allows us to understand and get through
all of those busy Friday afternoons
because in the end
don't we need these jobs
for more than just their money
don't we need these jobs
so that we can stand in front of mirrors
and look at ourselves
without feeling worthless
or disconnected
like a CEO must
like a President or Prime Minister must
like the head of an HR department must
don't we need these jobs
in the same way that Martin Luther King needed his dream
in the same way that Rosa Parks needed to stay on that bus
in the same way that the Wilding needed equality
that gravity
pulls on the planets and stars
the same way that the sea
can never stop being the sea

we all want to stay a part of this control room
for as long as possible
because this is where we learnt
that the men and women who are employed by Phoenix Express
are the same
as every working man
and woman
and that all of our fingertips combined
might just be the fingertips
that keep us and this Universe
stitched together

Acknowledgements

Thanks are due to the editors of the following, where some of these poems were first published – *Caja de resistencia, Culture Matters, I am not a silent poet, Ink Sweat & Tears, Militant Thistles, Mistress Quickly's Bed, Proletarian Poetry* and Martin Hayes, *The Things Our Hands Once Stood For* (Culture Matters/Manifesto Press, 2018).